"As the world keeps changing, you can either stay out in front and ride the change or get left behind. It's a binary outcome. The only way to be out front and succeed is by making a conscious decision to do so. This book will help you understand why and how, and smart people will read it."

— Brian Carruthers, best selling author of *Untrapped* and *Money Mindset*

"If the fast-changing world has you worried you'll get left behind, then read *The Relevance Gap*. This book will get you past self-imposed limitations and equip you with the skills necessary to stay relevant."

— Chris Widener, best-selling author of *The Art of Influence*

"Everyone of us experiences *The Relevance Gap* at some point in our lives. The challenge is knowing how to overcome the uncertainty and hesitation so that we can realize our potential in a rapidly changing world. Scott Scantlin has written an outstanding, practical book that will help you bridge the gap!"

— Steven Iwersen, CSP and author of
The Porcupine Principles: How to Move Prickly People to Preferred Outcomes

"The future doesn't have to be scary. *The Relevance Gap* helps you tap into abilities and talents you didn't even know you had so you'll be a powerhouse for decades to come."

— Tyler R. Tichelaar, PhD and award-winning author of *The Nomad Editor*

"This powerful and dynamic book helps you pinpoint and focus on what matters most in your life. Instead of trying to be all things to all people, the author shows you how to create an action plan to continuously improve and evaluate yourself. Based on simple and easy-to-implement practices, learned through trial and error, he shares tools that work to ensure you continuously resonate with what's important to you in an ever-changing landscape."

— Susan Friedmann, CSP, international bestselling author of
Riches in Niches: How to Make it BIG in a Small Market

THE
RELEVANCE

GAP

How to Stay Relevant and Thrive
in a Fast-Changing World

SCOTT SCANTLIN

AVIVA
PUBLISHING
New York

Published by:

Aviva Publishing
Lake Placid, NY, USA
(518) 523-1320
www.AvivaPubs.com

Address all inquiries to:

Scott Scantlin
6114 MO-9, Suite B6
Parkville, MO 64152
813-368-0833
Scottscan@gmail.com
ScottScantlin.com

ISBN: 978-1-950241-27-9
Library of Congress Control Number: 2019913475

Editors: Tyler Tichelaar and Larry Alexander, Superior Book Productions
Cover Design and Interior Book Layout: Meredith Lindsay, Mediamercantile.com
Author Photo Credit: Fernando Leon

Every attempt has been made to source properly all quotes.

This book is dedicated to my wife, Kim, who has been there with me and supported me over the years. She has been my loyal partner and my saving grace. Through thick and thin, good times and bad, she has never wavered, and for that I am eternally grateful. Without her, none of this would have been possible, and with her support, there is no limit. Thanks for always believing in me! We did it Babe!

CONTENTS

INTRODUCTION 9

CHAPTER ONE: The Relevance Gap 13

CHAPTER TWO: The Race for Relevance.. 21

CHAPTER THREE: Where You Are and Where You Could Be 35

CHAPTER FOUR: The Aggregation of Marginal Gains 45

CHAPTER FIVE: A Different Kind of Company 63

CHAPTER SIX: Developing Guiding Core Values................................... 71

CHAPTER SEVEN: Emotional Intelligence 85

CHAPTER EIGHT: Bio-Hacking Performance 95

CHAPTER NINE: The Power of Mindset.. 113

CHAPTER TEN: Cultivating Clarity 121

CHAPTER ELEVEN: Creating a Vision.. 129

CHAPTER TWELVE: The Power of Self-Talk 137

CHAPTER THIRTEEN: The Path to Your Inherent Ultimate Potential.... 149

CHAPTER FOURTEEN: Changing Our Preference and Patterns............. 159

CHAPTER FIFTEEN: Winning the Race for Relevance 165

A FINAL NOTICE: Do More Than Read This Book.............................. 167

RESOURCES 169

ABOUT THE AUTHOR 171

INTRODUCTION

The world around us is changing so fast that it seems impossible to keep up. It's as if there is a *gap* that's widening. It is the gap between where you are now and whether you will be relevant in the future. If you don't shore up the breaches, the gap will grow. Minding the gap leaves you with an overwhelming feeling that you have fallen too far behind to ever catch up.

You may be asking yourself how you got here. How did I fall so far behind? Why can't I find the motivation to change? When did I give up on my dreams? And, where do I start now?

A few years ago, I found myself facing a similar crisis and had to answer those questions. Through my journey, I quickly realized I had lost sight of the one thing that drives us all—our inherent potential. I had settled for a lesser version of myself and gotten caught in the trap of day-to-day routines. Sadly, with the whole world at our fingertips, losing sight of our inherent potential is easy to do, and we can spend our entire lives completely distracted, chasing someone else's dream.

To show you how to harness your potential and unleash your possibilities, I have written this book. To help you cross the gap one step at a time, I have broken this book down into manageable chapters. In addition, at the end of each chapter, I have included a summary and some steps to help you identify your potential and take action.

In Chapter 1 of *The Relevance Gap*, I define what the relevance gap is and how successful people use *the gap* to realize their potential and drive themselves on to new possibilities. Chapter 2 talks about how big business and industry leaders are responding to the relevance gap and some of the emerging trends shaping our culture and redefining the traditional employment model moving forward. Then, in Chapter 3, we will look at how to get from where you are to where you could be, and I'll share the formula I used to realize my potential and consider new possibilities.

In Chapter 4, we will review *The Aggregation of Marginal Gains*—how small improvements daily can quickly make up lost ground and carry you on to uncommon success. In Chapter 5, I will introduce you to *a different kind of company* that believes in the value of human dignity and making the world a better place by improving the lives of its employees and customers. In Chapter 6, we will get into the process of developing core values in alignment with your overall potential individually and corporately.

In Chapter 7, I will open your eyes to the importance of *Emotional Intelligence* and how to use it effectively to overcome disempowering beliefs and create new empowering beliefs that will serve you. In Chapter 8, we will get into some bio-hacking techniques that will give you the energy and focus you need to stay relevant and enhance performance. Then, in Chapter 9, through *The Power of Mindset*, I will show you how to condition your intentionality to move you toward your potential and manifest the vision you have created for your life.

In Chapter 10, we will clearly define *the gap* between where you are and where you could be, and we will review the steps necessary to stay relevant and achieve the vision you will create. In Chapter 11, we will shift to practical steps for creating a vision and setting goals. I will walk you through some key exercises you can use to find out what you really want most in life. In Chapter 12, we will review *The Power of Self-Talk* and how to shape your self-talk to move you toward your vision and goals.

In Chapter 13, we will uncover our deeper motivations and what our ultimate inherent potential is. In Chapter 14, I will show you how to reprogram your preferences and patterns to move you toward your potential. And in Chapter 15, I will share my final thoughts on how you too can win the race for relevance.

If you apply the steps and principles laid out in this book, you will re-discover your potential and bridge *the gap* from where you are to where you could be. You will overcome that feeling of falling behind and find a sense of certainty and confidence that you matter, you belong, and you can make a difference. Then you will be on your way to becoming the best version of yourself—who you were destined to be.

I have studied personal development for over twenty-five years, and the single biggest mistake I have made along the way is standing too long in someone else's shadow. Though I own multiple businesses and have served in various leadership roles over the years, I have found that I am not immune to change. I have learned that *success* is never owned, and there is no finish line. We are all subject to variables beyond our control, and the marketplace is not going to cater to our preferences. The truth is I don't have all the an-swers; I am still learning, but that's also the key to my success. A space exists deep inside all of us, put there by design, to drive us to become the best ver-sions of ourselves. This is the Gap, the gap you can never fill, that is always there driving you to seek new possibilities, driving you to become the person you are destined to be.

I understand why you have not pursued all your dreams, goals, and vi-sions. It is easy to get caught up in life's daily routines. Maybe you're a single mother or married with kids. Maybe you are the breadwinner in your fami-ly or taking care of aging parents. Maybe you've failed at something and lost hope. Somehow, life gets in the way, and you find yourself justifying the *sta-tus quo*. The responsibilities of life and work can be overwhelming, and we can lose sight of our dreams and goals. The good news is it's never too late. Don't waste your life as some passive spectator and neglect the dreams and visions you have for yourself. Your destiny was built by design, only for you to experience.

To truly unleash your potential and transform your life, you need a mentor: someone who has experience and can help you go from where you are to where you want to be. With your permission, I would like to be your coach. Throughout this book, I will guide you step-by-step in making that transformation and getting on a path to rediscovering your true potential. It is my goal that this book will encourage you, and millions of others around the world, to discover your true potential and inspire others around you to become the people they were destined to be.

Are you ready to go from where you are to where you could be? Are you ready to leave the *status quo* behind and discover your true potential? Are you ready to acquire some skills and techniques that can take you to a new level? If you are all in, let's get started and make this *journey* together. I believe in you! Let's go!

J. Scott Scantlin

CHAPTER ONE

The Relevance Gap

"For anyone to be successful, it is crucial that there exists within them the desire to be great or at least better than their current state. Without this desire, there would be no motivation or cause for action."

— Napoleon Hill

Never before in human history has there been more opportunity, more resources, and more options than we have today. With the explosion of the Internet, the entire world is at our fingertips. In the early '90s, we studied books like *The Roaring 2000s*, *The Popcorn Report*, and *Megatrends 2000* to try to get an idea of what the future might look like. Those books forecasted many of the things we see today, like live streaming, social media, the smartphone, and self-driving autonomous vehicles. At the time those books were published, the internet was in its infancy and most people didn't yet have access to it.

Today, we are all struggling just to keep up! Our lives are now interconnected through smartphones with more than 300 times the processing power of the world's fastest computer back in the '90s. Staying connected and plugged in to the world around us has never been more convenient; cloud-based computing has connected the entire world in a collective consciousness available at our fingertips. We have an app for everything, social media streams live on our phones 24/7, we can follow influencers on Twitter as posts go viral, and our news feeds bring the world to us in real-time. Our favorite movies, documentaries, and television programs are just a touch away on Hulu and Netflix. Video games are set in virtual realities. We can travel anywhere in the world using GPS, and dating websites are where we go to meet someone. It's all instant gratification, whatever we want, whenever we want it. Let's face the facts: Technology is not going away—it is speeding up.

The new economy is not going to go away, and you cannot afford to ignore it. What was once the technology revolution is now the marketplace. In fact, by the time you realize it, you are seriously behind. This is what I call *The Relevance Gap*: the distance between where you are and the speed of the world changing around you. The longer you wait to engage the new economy, the greater the gap. If you fall too far behind, you will become irrelevant in the marketplace. The good news is it's not all about technology. There is an old French proverb, "The more things change, the more they stay the same." Yes, technology is changing how we enter into the marketplace; however, the fundamentals of achieving success have not changed and never do.

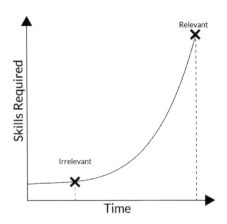

THE RELEVANCE GAP

The distance between where you are in relationship to the speed of the world changing around you.

The law of diminishing returns states that there is a point at which profits and/or benefits are outweighed by the amount of money and/or energy invested. We all have a winning formula, but despite our best efforts, as the world changes, our winning formula may no longer produce results. Too often, we do not realize the need for change and adaptation until it's too late. Staying busy doing what we have always done is not going to provide new outcomes. When we recognize that change and adaptation are necessary, it is critical that we evaluate where we are so we can adapt and expand into new opportunities.

THE LAW OF DIMINISHING RETURNS

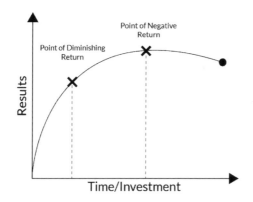

In recent years, top producers and industry leaders have struggled to stay relevant as technology and changes to delivery options have accelerated at a blistering pace. During the economic collapse of 2008, I watched many companies attempt to motivate their sales forces by offering cash bonuses, cars, exotic vacations, adjustments to compensation, or increased rewards for leaders at the top. No matter how much they threw at the field, it didn't seem to move the needle. Incentives don't drive change; potential does.

Doing what you have always done and expecting a different result kills opportunity. My grandmother is ninety-four years old. I once asked her "What's your secret?" She said, "Stay away from senior living facilities and never stop moving. When you stop moving, you die!" It is the same in your business and career—you are either expanding or contracting; there is no in between.

Have you stopped moving forward? Answer these questions:

- How long have you been at the same position?
- Have you tired of it or outgrown it?
- Do you feel excitement, or are you bored?
- Is it getting you up early and keeping you up late?
- Do you feel you have reached your capacity, or is there room for growth?

Your potential should be waking you up in the morning. When you are operating in tune with your potential, you have no need for an alarm clock. You wake up refreshed, with boundless energy, obsessed with only one thing. People who are driven by possibility take into consideration where they are, where they could be, and what their overall potential is in a given time frame. The chart below depicts this awareness. They also consider the long-term potential or capacity of what they endeavor to do.

EARNING POTENTIAL

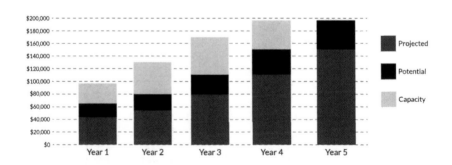

If you are not moving to the next level in your business or career, you have most likely come to a point where you are unwilling to do what is necessary to move forward, or you're just burned out. With success comes complacency. It's easy to get comfortable with success, a title, and a position. And though you may have the best intentions, you may lose sight of what you were fighting for in the first place.

The Potential Gap

To succeed, you have to get to a place where you no longer need rewards to motivate you. You don't need the house, the cars, the vacations. Your aboutness—the potential of who you are becoming and the difference you will make—will push you. Successful people don't measure success based on what they have done; they measure success against their potential. When successful people see their potential isn't lining up with their opportunities, they grow frustrated and become restless. Successful people recognize the gap between where they are and where they could be and allow that frustration and restlessness to drive them.

I have found that average people are not driven by potential; they are driven by consequences. They make a series of poor choices, without giving any consideration to the effect it's having on their future. It is the difference between being open-minded or empty-minded. Open-minded people are always considering the possibilities around them and giving potential opportunities a chance to grow or expand. Empty-minded people shut out possibilities and get stuck in the trap of their consequences. When the consequences of inaction catch up with their empty-mindedness, they are suddenly motivated and consider other possibilities.

This complacency is why the middle class is so vulnerable—they have a *status quo* mentality. They do just enough to live in a nice neighborhood with good schools, drive nice cars, and put some money away in their 401K. By the time they realize they are falling behind in the race for relevance, they will look for another way to do just enough to maintain the status quo, and by then, it's usually too late. You would think that potential would be the greater motivator, but in my experience, most people aren't driven by potential—they are driven by consequences.

If this is true, then being driven by your consequences is not going to sustain you long. People who are driven by circumstance alone will stop running the minute they outrun the consequences of their choices. A vast difference exists between having a burning desire to succeed or just trying to outrun your consequences. Consequences happen when you stay at a job you hate for thirty years. Most of us have been conditioned by our environment to do just enough to get by. To truly get motivated and live your dreams, you have to move beyond your circumstances and develop your intentionality so you can focus on your potential.

"Intentionality" is a mental state of directed thought that governs the intellectual or emotional tension between where you are and the potential of where you could be.

To deny your intentionality is to deny the essence of who you were created to be. You will never know true happiness until you find your true intentionality.

Do you feel you have potential greater than where you are right now?

People with highly developed intentionality don't read books and go to seminars for the entertainment. They read books and go to seminars because they are looking for the missing piece of the puzzle, the key that is going to unlock the vault and allow them to use their gifts. They have a desire to see their hopes and dreams become their reality, and they feel a sense of duty and obligation to see it through.

A case in point is Denzel Washington, winner of three Golden Globe awards, a Tony, and two Oscars. Recently, I saw Washington interviewed by Jamie Foxx. Foxx said to him, "When I watch your movies, a person who has done so much, it feels like you could just shut it down?" Washington responds, "It's not a competition, and I'm not competing against others. I'm just trying to get better. That's why I act on stage, act in movies, direct, and produce…because I like a challenge." Clearly, Washington doesn't need the money or another award to complete him. He is a master of his craft and wants to use his gifts to reach his potential.

Summary

The longer you wait to engage the new economy, the greater the gap. If you fall too far behind, you will become irrelevant in the marketplace. When you recognize that change and adaptation are necessary, it is critical to evaluate where you are so you can adapt and expand into new opportunities. To truly get motivated and live your dreams, you have to move beyond your circumstances and develop your intentionality; then you can focus on your potential.

Action Steps

Take a minute to evaluate where you are in relation to where you could be. Spend some time to consider your vulnerabilities and what needs to change for you to stay relevant in your job or your business. Then, make a list of things you love about what you do. Lastly, identify the *potential* and the *capacity* of your position or business.

Resources

For additional tools and training, visit TheRelevanceGap.com. To book Scott for an event or consultation, visit ScottScantlin.com. For free tips and motivation, follow him on Twitter and Facebook, and subscribe to his YouTube Channel @ScottScan1.

CHAPTER TWO

The Race for Relevance

"Two roads diverged in a wood, and I—I took the one less traveled by, and that has made all the difference."

— Robert Frost

When someone says, "My thing is," I know I am about to hear their firmly held opinions and excuses about why they don't want to do something. The truth, however, is they're falling behind. I recently attended an event for professional speakers called Video Intensive. This interactive event was designed to enable professional speakers to use video to engage audiences, get booked, and create new revenue for their businesses. Being the new guy in the room, I quickly realized everyone there was a little overwhelmed by how far behind they were. Just a few years earlier, the majority of revenue for speakers came from booking keynotes. Today, the number one revenue source for speakers is producing online courses. Times have changed in our respective fields, and we are all racing to stay relevant.

I remember a time when there was no internet, no mobile devices, and if you wanted something, you couldn't just order it on Amazon. We didn't have little communities with walkability, restaurants, and a Sprouts Farmers Market. I got a job before I turned eighteen so I could buy a car. Today, members of Generation Z may never need a driver's license. Instead, they use rideshares like Uber or Lyft. When I graduated from high school, I was expected to enroll in college. Today, college tuition is skyrocketing, and Gen Z feels college might not be the best route. Instead, they're getting degrees online, and they are more focused on entrepreneurship. When I finished college, if you wanted to start a business, you needed a substantial loan from a bank; today, Millennials and Gen Z can create an online venture and reach an audience of potential customers with a few hundred dollars and a Twitter account.

This generation isn't experiencing the same social and economic discomfort as earlier generations. Today, we are all living in this synthetic Utopia where basic needs are mostly met. We all have iPhones and flat screens. We are all interconnected on the web and social media. The speed of technology is creating a world where we don't experience the same struggle to survive that we did back in the '80s and '90s.

With the world at their fingertips, this generation of consumers isn't driven by survival or the need for extreme wealth. They are interested in belonging, community, and making a difference in the world. If you want to do business with Millennials and/or Gen Z, you must adapt to their communication preferences and get behind products and services that serve causes they support. They get behind brands that show support for issues they care about and will stop doing business with companies that behave in a way that doesn't line up with their values. By 2020, Gen Z will account for about 40 percent of all customers, and they're prepared to speak with their dollars.

Considering the rapid change of the last ten years, and how quickly the new generation is coming up behind us, it is imperative that we assimilate to the new economy and start picking up some skills that will move us toward the new potential. Millennials were the first generation introduced to social media, and Gen Z was the first generation to be raised on it.

You have to know how to use social media if you are going to reach these groups. Gen Z members have short attention spans and prefer video—so does everyone else. You need to learn how to use video platforms like YouTube, Facebook, Instagram, Snapchat, and LinkedIn if you are going to be relevant to the next generation of consumers.

If you want to attract talent, you need to get behind the causes that talent cares about and make room for them to participate in your business so they have some skin in the game. Collaborate with them and make them shareholders. Learn from their social media skills, and help them share the things they care about to an extensive global network. Building a company and ensuring a company's future are no longer just based on the bottom line—they're about making the world a better place. This is the best way to build a business. Consider how you can make a positive difference that supports your values; find a way to package that and you can profit financially from doing something you feel has value. The more money you make, the more significant your influence will be on the world around you.

Spending Billions

Major corporations are spending billions to compete with emerging startups in the race for relevance. Disruptive innovation is challenging established business models while presenting new opportunities. However, those opportunities require high-risk calculations if you want to stay relevant in the mobile app economy.

A great example of the Race for Relevance is the rideshare company Uber. This disruptive innovator has up-ended transportation and changed the way cities work around the world. Uber is spending billions in the race to capture the rideshare market globally. In 2018, Uber lost $1.8 billion on revenues of $11.3 billion, and it's not alone. Tech companies and startups across the globe are attracting venture capitalists and big investment firms willing to gamble on owning future markets through new technologies and market disruption. Recently, Uber took steps toward one of the most anticipated initial public offerings in years, one that could value the company at around $120 billion. If its gamble pays off, the move would reverberate around the globe, solidifying the company's position as one of the most significant technology firms of the past decade.

Author, leadership speaker, and business owner Grant Cardone always says, "Spend the money; own the space." Uber's CEO, Dara Khosrowshahi, agrees. In a letter accompanying the IPO's prospectus, he wrote: "We will not shy away from making short-term financial sacrifices where we see clear long-term benefits." Uber started in the depths of a financial crisis, with no existing market, and in the space of a decade, changed the rideshare transportation industry. In the short term, it may appear Uber is not set to turn a profit; however, with the prospect of autonomous vehicles, delivery services, and private and public transpiration, this CEO and Uber's investors are taking a calculated risk in the race for relevance in the twenty-first century.

Ford Motor Company faced the same challenges in the early stages of the automobile industry. In 1896, Henry Ford had enough time and money to devote attention to his personal experiments on gasoline engines, which culminated in the completion of his first self-propelled vehicle. Encouraged by Thomas Edison, Ford designed and built a second vehicle in 1898. Backed by the capital of Detroit lumber baron, William H. Murphy, Ford founded the Detroit Automobile Company in August 1899. Due to high prices and low quality, the company didn't last long, dissolving in January 1901.

Ford would go through a series of partnerships, investors, and lawsuits before his big break came from the most unlikely of places. Large cities all around the world were "drowning in horse manure." Cities at the time were dependent on thousands of horses for transporting both people and goods. At the time, more than 11,000 hansom cabs were on the streets of London alone. Several thousand horse-drawn buses, each needing twelve horses, made a staggering total of more than 50,000 horses transporting people around the city each day. Even more horse-drawn carts and drays were delivering goods around what was then the world's largest city.

All these horses created significant problems. The main concern was the manure left on the streets. On average, a horse will produce between fifteen and thirty-five pounds of manure per day, so you can imagine the sheer scale of the problem. The manure also attracted a lot of flies, which spread typhoid fever and other diseases. Each horse also produced about two pints of urine per day, and to make things worse, the average life expectancy for a working horse was only about three years. Horse carcasses, therefore, also had to be removed from the streets. The bodies were often left to decay so the corpses could be more easily sawed into pieces for removal. Nor was this just London's problem. New York had a population of 100,000 horses producing around 2.5 million pounds of manure a day.

The problem came to a head in 1894 when *The Times*, the London-based newspaper, predicted, "In fifty years, every street in London will be buried under nine feet of manure." The situation became known as the "Great Horse Manure Crisis of 1894."

The situation was debated in 1898 at the world's first international urban planning conference, held in New York, but no solution was found. It seemed urban civilization was doomed. However, necessity is the mother of invention, and the invention, in this case, was the horseless carriage.

Henry Ford found a way to produce cars faster and at an affordable price, introducing the Model T to the world in 1908. The car was affordable, easy to drive, and cheap to repair. In 1913, Ford introduced the assembly line, which enabled Ford to build cars faster and at a more affordable price. In 1916, the price dropped to $360, and by 1918, half of all cars in America were Model Ts. In cities all around the globe, horses were replaced and motorized vehicles became the primary source of transport. In the span of a decade, this seemingly impossible problem had been resolved. Henry Ford had transformed the transportation industry.

Will Uber succeed in transforming the transportation industry again? We will find out soon in the race for relevance!

The Age of Disruption

Disruption has become the expression used to describe a period of transformational change like the world has never seen. The term "disruption" has moved into the everyday vocabulary of media pundits, political scientists, and corporate strategists.

However, what exactly does it mean to live in the age of disruption? The creation of the World Wide Web was the starting point for a digital revolution that has dramatically changed every aspect of our daily lives. Social media has reduced the world to the size of a keypad on our mobile device. Through social media, we have reconnected with lifelong friends and shared life-changing experiences. Social media has also allowed us to engage with communities of common interest, as well as greatly divide us through the polarization of our politics.

In the growing realm of social media and digital content, disruption has penetrated every area of society, causing a rapid change and acceleration in business, education, and politics. It has also led to new alliances as content providers look to collaborate and better position themselves in the world of mobile apps and live streaming.

Disruption has leveled the playing field for innovators and entrepreneurs wanting to compete with big business. Many startups have been able to enter the market and compete directly for the same customers, creating competition. The future of artificial intelligence, nanotechnology, 3D printing, autonomous vehicles, and blockchain does not belong to big business; it belongs to the creators of disruptive innovation who make things simpler, easier, and more affordable. For example, Netflix owns no movie theaters, Uber owns no taxi cabs, Airbnb owns no hotels, and LegalShield owns no law firms, yet they are dominating their market categories. What do they all have in common? They are disruptive, technology-based companies that connect the consumer to the product through a mobile app. Like Amazon, which owns no bookstores, these technology-based companies are transforming the marketplace by meeting the consumer where they are, on their mobile device.

In the wake of disruptive innovation also comes displacement. While competition has allowed markets to expand and grow, we have also seen those who failed to embrace change forced into mergers or bankruptcy. Many companies are thinning retail locations and adjusting their models to stay profitable and compete. In the years ahead, disruptive innovation has the potential to threaten the relevance and survival of any business.

To stay relevant and thrive in the Age of Disruption, you must upgrade your skills and embrace change. Gone is the safety and security of the *status quo*. Doing just enough isn't going to cut it. You want to operate from a position of strategy, not survival. It is always best to upgrade your skills and reinvent yourself when you have time on your side. Don't wait until you are faced with a crisis to embrace change. In the Age of Disruption, you have two choices: embrace change, or face the consequences of neglect.

The Employment Gap

The so called "Silver Tsunami" represents serious challenges ahead in the Age of Disruption. Every day, 10,000 Baby Boomers turn sixty-five. They currently represent one out of four employed workers in the United States. Many continue to work out of necessity. The fallout of the financial crisis of 2008 left many with debt and depleted retirement savings. In addition, people are living longer and enjoy the social aspect of having a job.

Since the 1920s, the lifespan of the average business has dropped from sixty-seven years to only fifteen years; consequently, whether you are a Millennial seeking purpose or a Boomer who wants to stay productive, the threat of the "Employment Gap" looms for all generations.

A gap in employment history is important because it raises red flags in the eyes of a potential employer when the unemployed individual tries to return to work. In worst-case scenarios, you can become unemployable in your field. Even in best-case scenarios, you will undoubtedly take a salary cut and find yourself reporting to someone who would formerly have reported to you.

Lacking the skills necessary to perform and compete in the Age of Disruption could devastate your career. If you're not careful, even a couple of years as a stay-at-home parent without keeping your employable skills updated could cost you. Can you imagine a computer programmer finding a new position after five years outside the workforce?

In the Age of Disruption, the greater the employment gap, the harder it is to keep or find employment. Even more at risk are older workers who may be stereotyped as less flexible, less motivated, or too slow to learn or keep up with new technology and changes in the workplace. If you are an aging worker, you cannot afford to fall behind. Keeping abreast of your field every year is the best way to stay employable at something you like doing.

The Side Hustle

Employment gaps are a perfect time for pursuing career options and discovering more about yourself and your interests. Many people are turning to online courses to acquire the necessary skills or earn a much-needed degree. Alternatively, you may decide to change careers altogether and go after your dreams.

Many Americans are even taking on a side hustle to make ends meet. According to a new Bankrate survey, 45 percent of working Americans earn extra income on top of their regular jobs. Not surprisingly, this trend is most common among Millennials, with 48 percent doing some side work. Meanwhile, 39 percent of Gen Xers have a side gig, as do 28 percent of Baby Boomers.

One of the critical principles of generating wealth and security in the Age of Disruption is having multiple streams of income. The survey found that people in wealthier households are more likely to have a side gig, with 43 percent of households earning at least $80,000 per year having a side hustle. If you are looking for a career change or want to chase your dreams, 27 percent of those surveyed say they are more passionate about their side gig than their primary job or career.

However, even if incomes are going up, expenses seem to be going up even faster. Three in ten working Americans with a side hustle say they need the extra income to help cover the cost of regular living expenses.

Americans working a side gig spend an average of twelve hours per week working on their side hustle and earn an average of $1,122 per month. For households in need of additional income, that amount of money can be significant.

Due to the ever-changing nature of jobs and stagnant wages, young people have turned to side hustles to generate needed income, maintain their skills, or repay student loans. Moreover, younger adults rely on side gigs to provide a larger portion of their income. About 40 percent of Millennials with a side hustle say it's the source of at least half of their monthly earnings.

The side hustle has become its own industry. There are emerging businesses that provide a platform for you to plug into and work when you want to and contract your employable skills for hire. Side hustles vary in earning potential. Some pay just $10 an hour, while others can pay over $50 an hour. For example, pet sitting often pays about $10 an hour. Alternatively, other side gigs require a lot of dedication and effort. Freelance writing, for example, can be a lucrative side business, but you have to meet tight deadlines and handle demanding clients.

One benefit of having a side hustle is the flexibility to scale your hours up and down. Side gigs like Uber and Lyft allow you to set your own schedule and decide when you want to work. For example, if you have some unexpected expenses and money is tight, as a driver for Uber or Lyft, you can turn on your ride share app and make extra income that day. On the other hand, when you don't need the extra money or you're stressed with work, you can reduce your side gig workload and take a break. If you are starting your own work-from-home business or you are a freelance contractor between gigs, driving for Uber or Lyft can be a lifesaver.

While you can start a side gig on your own, the process can be time consuming. It can take a while to build up your clientele and become profitable. If you're already tight on money, consider working a side gig using a ready-made app like Uber, Lyft, Turo, Amazon Flex, Postmates, Door Dash, Shipt, VRBO, Handy, Wag, Dolly, Zeel, etc. Companies like these connect you with customers and allow you to start making money right away. The apps handle marketing, customer outreach, and invoicing. This eliminates overhead costs and administrative tasks so you can focus your efforts on your side hustle.

Rise of the Freelance Contract Worker

In the Age of Disruption, we have witnessed the growth of the freelance contract worker, a new kind of employment arrangement where skilled labor is contracted to a potential employer without constraints, benefits, or full-time employment. A new NPR/Marist poll finds that one in five jobs in America is held by a worker under contract. Within a decade, contractors and freelancers could make up half of the American workforce.

A vast majority of freelancers are free agents by choice. In many cases, people find "alternative work arrangements" because they best suit their needs. For example, a young couple or single parent needs a work-from home gig so they can stay home with their new baby. Alternatively, freelancers may find their work commute unreasonable or find it too difficult to relocate for a better job. In many cases, they don't like the constraints of traditional employment and are even willing to take a pay cut for more flexibility to chase their dreams.

According to the NRP/Marist poll:
- Twenty percent of all American workers are contract workers hired to work on a specific project or for a fixed period.
- Fifty-one percent of contract workers don't receive benefits.
- Forty-nine percent of contract workers have income that varies from month to month or seasonally.
- Sixty-five percent of contract workers are male, and 62 percent are under forty-five.

- Sixty-six percent of part-time workers prefer that kind of schedule.
- Fifty-six percent of workers received a raise in the past year.
- Eighty-four percent of workers are not worried that they will lose their job in the next year.
- Fifty-four percent of workers think it would be difficult to relocate for a better job.

These statistics are emblematic of the kind of contract work expanding into every corner of the economy. Technology is automating basic tasks, and employers need specialized expertise on demand. Freelance contractors are hired by the hour or by the task, allowing the employer the flexibility to size up or down. Online platforms like Upworks and Fiver match freelance workers with clients. It's like dating profiles—but with customer reviews and billing assistance. There are even industry-specific platforms allowing businesses to narrow their search and respond quickly to this ever-growing demand for contract workers.

Contract work is today's economic reality. The freelance market may soon replace the traditional resume for those seeking full-time employment. Contracting allows employers to test workers who are ultimately hoping to land full-time positions with benefits.

Arun Sundararajan, a management professor at New York University and author of *The Sharing Economy*, says, "This is the work arrangement for the future." The new normal will be freelance work. "Twenty years from now, I don't think a typical college graduate is going to expect that full-time employment is their path to building a career."

In the past year, I hired a part-time, twenty-hours-a-week person who was very talented but needed thirty hours, so we gave her the thirty hours and hired her for the position. A year later, we moved her off the thirty-hours-per-week schedule and made her a freelance contractor. Her work is mostly automated, so we set her up with the resources she needs to work from her home. With our new arrangement, she now logs work during available hours and has the flexibility she needs to pursue other sources of income. She now has the option to market her freelance skills or search for part-time or full-time positions with benefits while staying under contract with us.

In the "alternative work arrangement," the responsibility of handling saving for retirement and healthcare shifts to contract workers. Some people, despite their best efforts, just aren't going to be successful in doing that. However, the idea of getting your pension check every year from your company is not realistic either. There will need to be a safety net, but we will leave that to the policymakers.

The idea of being responsible for your retirement, healthcare, and taxes may be unsettling or a bit overwhelming. However, you cannot afford to stick your head in the sand and hope the world goes away. Instead of ignoring inevitable change, you should embrace change and get out in front of it. Start now by identifying some of your marketable skills and set up your profile with Upworks or Fiver. If you are in a technical field, you may want to find an industry-specific platform on which to place your profile and see if you can land some freelance work.

The free enterprise system has a way of creating consequential change that forces us out of our comfort zone and moves us in a new direction with new opportunities and potential. Despite our expectations or disappointments, there is always a silver lining. You may find your dream job, excel in a newfound profession, enjoy the freedom of flexibility, increase your income, or form multiple streams of income. You may find the enjoyment of productivity or the impact of purpose intoxicating. Regardless of our best-laid plans, change is inevitable, and it will be the free enterprise system that will pave the way forward in the emerging employment model of the freelance contract worker.

Summary

Lacking the skills necessary to perform and compete in the Age of Disruption could devastate a career. To stay relevant and thrive in the Age of Disruption, it is imperative to assimilate to the new economy and start picking up some skills that will move you toward new potential. In the growing realm of social media and digital content, disruption has penetrated every area of society, causing a rapid change and acceleration in business, education, and politics. While competition has allowed markets to expand and grow, those who have neglected the need to adapt may have to face the consequences in a fast-changing world. Instead of ignoring the inevitable, we should get out in front of it.

Action Steps

Start by identifying some of your marketable skills, and set up your profile with Upworks or Fiver. If you like where you are and want to stay on or advance with your current employer, join a trade association specific to your profession. Attend its meetings and conferences. Also, take online courses where you can upgrade your skills. Report to your employer what you have learned and get feedback on how to improve your position. Lastly, pick up a side hustle where you can earn while you learn. You never know—you may just discover a passion that takes you to a new level of potential!

Resources

For additional tools and training, visit TheRelevanceGap.com. To book Scott for an event or consultation, visit ScottScantlin.com. For free tips and motivation, follow him on Twitter and Facebook, and subscribe to his YouTube Channel @ScottScan1.

CHAPTER THREE

Where You Are and Where You Could Be

"I don't think I have made it by any means because I measure against my potential."

— Grant Cardone

Subprime Meltdown

Before the subprime mortgage meltdown of 2006, my marketing business was expanding across North America. I was recognized nationally as a company leader and spoke at regional and national events. I liked my position, my titles, and my success. Then one night, while presenting to a large audience, I heard this voice inside say, "Is this it? Is this all there is?" I had reached the top and was no longer satisfied with the results. That night, I realized I would not reach my potential if I kept doing just enough to stay where I was.

Before I got the chance to realize my potential, Lehman Brothers fell, followed by a complete collapse of the economy. Business slowed and my income was cut in half. Within a few years, I moved back to Kansas City and fell apart. I could not find my way. There was no level of effort, no magic pixie dust I could sprinkle that would revive my failing business. Changing the compensation plan, bonuses, incentives, lowering rates—nothing changed the outcome. Simply put, I became irrelevant. Maybe you can relate.

With the world changing around me so quickly, how the hell was I going to keep up? The funny thing was people were thriving in our company, so if I were going to turn my life around, I needed to reinvent myself. I stepped out of leadership, scaled back interaction with my team, and leased a small office. This allowed me the space I needed to reevaluate my business without obligations and distractions. I needed a new plan, so I set about reevaluating my potential.

Below are the three primary steps I used to evaluate my short-term potential and my long-term capacity:

1. **Evaluate Potential:** Away from the noise, I was able to take inventory of where I was and consider where I could be. I needed to verify that the company's model was in alignment with my vision, so I revisited why I got started with my company to begin with. I wanted to get out in front of a business that offered a new product or service that everyone needed, very few people owned, was subscription-based, and paid monthly residuals. I also wanted the option to create override commissions by building sales teams. I also needed to know I could make a living marketing the services directly to consumers. Though the company had been through a lot of changes, these core values were still intact.

2. **Consider the Requirements**—The next thing I did was consider the income potential—what was the most reliable return on investment? To me, the most substantial return was a satisfied customer, and recognizing that return was based on customer longevity. In our business, it's called retention. Some customers have more staying power than others, so I made an evaluation and decided to focus my efforts on markets with the highest rate of retention. Entering into new markets required new skills, associations, and activities. Since I had considered the short-term potential and the long-term capacity, I was fully prepared to accept the new requirements.

3. **Willing to Do What's Necessary**—There is only one gear in necessity—*all-out-massive action*! You must generate a lot of thrust and get altitude quickly to achieve your desired outcome. Being accountable and modeling successful people who are doing what is needed to achieve what you desire is the fastest way to get results. I chose role models working in the markets I was targeting who had the success I desired and the income I wanted. I enrolled in training, jumped on conference calls, drove into regional events, and flew out to conventions where I could learn from the best of the best. I learned their language, dressed like them, read the same books they were reading, and registered for the same events. If you want results, you have to do what is necessary to achieve those results. To be successful, you must be coachable, willing to work, and have a burning desire to succeed. I was willing to travel, get the training, get out in the field, go back for more training, and repeat the process until I achieved my desired results.

Through this process, I completely rewrote my business strategy and learned an entirely new skill set, and it was working. Within two years, I doubled my income. With positive results and mastery of new skills, I began to realize my new business was scalable, so I moved into a bigger office and started recruiting associates. I am currently adding new accounts and associates at an incredible pace and looking for more office space to facilitate our growth. With my new model, and my willingness to do what is necessary, I could scale my business beyond my current capacity and earn over $1,000,000 a year in residual income.

Gauging Your Capacity for Growth

During the NFL draft, scouts and coaches consider the players' capacity and potential. The coaching staff knows that once the player is drafted, the system will give the coaching staff an idea of the player's capacity. When the Chiefs drafted Patrick Mahomes back in 2017, they had a sense of his potential; however, since then this player's capacity has been off the charts. In his first full year under center, Mahomes threw more than fifty touchdowns, was named NFL most valuable player, and took the Kansas City Chiefs to their first playoff win in twenty-four years: the AFC West Championship!

Whether professional athletes, business owners, corporate executives, or sales professionals, we all have potential and capacity. Many times, the size of our role does not equal the size of our ability. When our role limits our potential, we grow restless. Then our intuition or gut feeling tells us it is time to move on or acquire new skills to move us to a higher capacity. We all know that if you stay too long in your current role, you will stagnate and get stuck in a position you are not meant to fill. If you want to remain relevant in the marketplace, it is vital to consider the capacity of your current role and ensure it lines up with your potential and ability to do and be more.

Back on that night when, during a presentation, I thought to myself, *Is this it?* I realized if I just kept doing enough to stay where I was, I would never reach my potential. Sometimes we get caught up in our identity along the way and lose sight of the bigger picture. When I got involved in my business, I saw it as a vehicle for one day becoming a professional speaker. Though my business allowed me to present to broad audiences regularly, the stage I was on was not big enough for my purpose.

Sadly, most of us are just trying to figure out how to repeat the numbers we hit the month before. We do just enough to maintain the *status quo*, the annual vacation, the bonus check, the car bonus. We start our year with the best of intentions, and by June, we are consumed with summer vacation, kids out of school, and every other excuse to explain why we are settling for average.

The founder of LegalShield, Harland Stonecipher, used to say, "There is nothing older than yesterday's sales numbers." High achievers are never satisfied with mediocre numbers. Average numbers yield average results. High achievers don't make excuses or justify empty-minded thinking. They always consider their potential and work tirelessly to close the gap between where they are and where they could be. If you can relate, you may be feeling frustrated, restless, or unsettled. These are the signs that you are a high achiever who is off course and has stayed too long at your current level—you've lost your intentionality. When you are off course, you are off purpose, and you are drifting away from your potential.

To realize your capacity, you must develop your intentionality and become a "capacity thinker." Average people are what I call "surface thinkers." They cannot see past the screen on their mobile device. They spend their lives caged by their emotional reaction to everything they see on the surface.

Capacity thinkers see things from 10,000 feet up looking down. They can see ten to twenty years out and consider how their potential will grow and develop over time. Capacity thinkers see problems and events on the surface as an opportunity to overcome challenges. They understand the big picture and have plans to grow and develop their skills as a leader and visionary. They surround themselves with successful people and staff their team with like-minded individuals who share their vision. Their organization is built around personal development and growth, and it is made up of open-minded individuals who can get the job done. Capacity thinkers make a huge investment in their personal growth and invest in the development and growth of their team. They see their staff as *stakeholders* and get *emotional buy-in* from their team.

The Four Drivers of Capacity

When someone has reached their capacity, they feel as though they have arrived; then everything seems to flow effortlessly, almost to a fault. But if you are not careful, you may slip into a pattern of complacency where you are no longer challenged by your capacity's potential and lose sight of your intentionality.

To cultivate your intentionality, you need to revisit your aboutness and directedness. What is important to you? What are you about? If you can discover what's important to you, what you are about, and attach the meaning of who you are to what you are producing, it naturally motivates you to expand your capacity.

To rediscover what's important, we need to revisit the four primary motivators that drive us.

1. **Consequences:** Cause and effect. What are the consequences of taking action on new potential, and what are the consequences of not taking action? You are either expanding or contracting; there is no in between.

2. **Lifestyle:** New potential and new capacity bring opportunities for a new lifestyle, where the consequences of not moving to the next level of your capacity will eventually result in downgrading your lifestyle.

3. **Potential:** Having the capacity to become or develop into something in the future. Your potential is the primary motivator, the centerpiece of your intentionality.

4. **Purpose:** The reason for which something is created or exists. Your purpose is the ultimate outcome of who you are becoming. Your intuition is a gut feeling that tells you there is a big picture behind who you are and what you are about. If you reach for your potential, it will lead you to your purpose.

Evaluating Your Growth Potential

When talking with people about the reason they want to start a new business, I hear things like, "I hate my job," "I want to travel," "I have no retirement," or "I want something to do when I retire." What they are really saying is they want freedom, but are they willing to pay the price?

Freedom is not free; it is an endless fight! If you want freedom, you have to know the requirements and be willing to do what is necessary to achieve it. Average people are unwilling to do what is required to reach their potential. They are satisfied with a home in a subdivision, a mid-size car, an annual vacation, and a 401K. They have a nine-to-five mindset and are happy with the *status quo*. They have traded their freedom for comfort and their potential for a cookie-cutter idea of the American Dream.

Successful people feel caged by comfort. They are not interested in comfort; they are interested in their potential. Ben Bolt, my mentor in my early years, always used to say, "Successful people like pleasing results; unsuccessful people like pleasing habits." Successful people have a different kind of appetite; they aren't satisfied with the *status quo*. They know there is room for growth, and they are driven by a fire inside that says they can do more—they can be more!

Every position, job title, or business model has a minimum and maximum income potential based on our level of effort, ability, skill, or experience. The eternal optimist would tell us the possibilities are infinite. But since we are finite creatures, income potential or capacity may be limited by things beyond our control, like market location, business model, etc.

The only variable we have control over is choice. If I am going to invest my skills, talent, and passion into a vehicle (promotion, business model, or marketing project), I want to make sure it lines up with my intentionality and can produce the results I am looking for. In other words, "Is the juice worth the squeeze?"

Ask yourself these questions:
- What will the requirements be?
- What is my short-term potential?
- What is the minimum and maximum income potential?
- Does it line up with my vision?
- Does the timing work?
- What is the lifespan of the opportunity?

In his book *Eat That Frog*, Brian Tracy tells a story about crossing a stretch of the Sahara Desert. The desert was 500 miles across without any food or water available that entire distance. It was totally flat, like a sand parking lot that stretched to the horizon in all directions. More than 1,300 people had perished crossing that particular stretch of the Sahara. Often, drifting sands obliterated the track across the desert, and travelers got lost in the night. To overcome the lack of features in the terrain, the French had marked the track with black, fifty-five-gallon oil drums, five kilometers apart, at exactly the earth's curvature. Wherever you were in the daytime, you could see two oil barrels—the one you just passed and the one five kilometers ahead. All you had to do was steer for the next oil barrel. As a result, Tracy was able to cross the biggest desert in the world by simply taking it "one oil barrel at a time."

Chasing a vision is somewhat like seeing a mirage in the desert—you can't quite make it out, but it continues to draw you forward. If you are not careful, you will get off track and find yourself lost in the night with nothing to guide you. You need to evaluate your vision and make sure the barrel ahead leads to your destination. If you get started with a position, new marketing project, or a business model, you want to ensure it fits with the intentionality of your long-term vision. Your job is to go as far as you can see, until you can see far enough to go even farther.

Summary

If you're going to stay relevant, it is best to upgrade your skills and reinvent yourself when you have time on your side. You are subject to change and variables that are beyond your control. It's easy to get caught up in the day-to-day routines of the status quo and get blindsided by consequences of inaction. To create lasting transformational change requires a conscious effort on your part.

We all have unmet potential, and many times the size of our role does not equal the size of our ability. When our role limits our potential, it is time to move on or acquire new skills to move us to a higher capacity. If you stay too long in your current role, you may end up in a position you are not meant to fill. If you want to remain relevant in the marketplace, it is vital to consider the capacity of your current role and ensure it lines up with your potential and ability to do and be more.

Action Steps

Spend some time evaluating your current role. Ask yourself if the income potential is lining up with your level of ability, skill, or experience. If you have not reached the capacity of your role, then take the steps suggested in this book to acquire new skills and experiences that will level you up to your capacity. If you have surpassed your role's capacity, then it is time to take the next step and level up your career. To do this, reevaluate your potential, consider what the requirements will be, and be prepared to do what is necessary to achieve it.

Resources

For additional tools and training, visit TheRelevanceGap.com. To book Scott for an event or consultation, visit ScottScantlin.com. For free tips and motivation, follow him on Twitter and Facebook, and subscribe to his You-Tube Channel @ScottScan1.

CHAPTER FOUR

The Aggregation of Marginal Gains

"Forget about perfection; focus on progression and compound the improvements."

— Sir David John Brailsford

Team Sky

Sir David John Brailsford is a British cycling coach, the former performance director of British Cycling, and the current general manager of Team Sky, a British professional cycling team that competes at the UCI World Team level. In 1996, the British Cycling team was a national embarrassment. Broke and lacking equipment, Britain introduced a national lottery to help fund Olympic sports.

At the time, professional cyclists in Great Britain had endured nearly 100 years of mediocrity and had almost no record of success. Since 1908, British riders had won just a single gold medal at the Olympics, and they had fared even worse in cycling's biggest race, the Tour de France. When Sir Dave was appointed performance director in 2003, no British cyclist had ever won the Tour De France in its 100-year history. In fact, the performance of British riders was such an embarrassment to the sport that one of the top bike manufacturers in Europe refused to sell bikes to the team because it was afraid doing so would damage the brand and hurt sales.

With public financing in place through the national lottery, the team secured new equipment and moved to a state-of-the-art velodrome in Manchester. At the 2004 Olympic Games, Great Britain won two cycling gold medals. Under Brailsford's leadership, the cycling team continued to improve, winning multiple world championships in road, track, BMX, and mountain bike racing. Great Britain led the cycling medal table at the 2008 and 2012 Olympic Games, winning eight golds at both events, while British cyclists won fifty-nine world championships across different disciplines from 2003 to 2013. Brailsford also became the manager of the British-based professional cycling team known as Team Sky, leading it to victories in the Tour de France in 2012, 2013, 2015, 2016, 2017, and 2018.

With success comes accusations, so the team was tested for performance-enhancing drugs. With no evidence of drugs or doping, the cycling world wanted to know what methods and philosophy Sir Dave used to helped the Brits achieve international domination in one of the world's most competitive sports.

What made Brailford different from previous coaches was his fascination with kaizen and other process-improvement techniques he discovered while studying for his MBA. It struck Brailford that we should think small, not big, and adopt a philosophy of continuous improvement through the "aggregation of marginal gains," which is the philosophy of searching for a tiny margin of improvement in everything you do. Sir Dave said, "The whole principle came from the idea that if you broke down everything you could think of that goes into riding a bike and then improve each bit by 1 percent, you will get a significant increase when you put them all together."

THE AGGREGATION OF MARGINAL GAINS

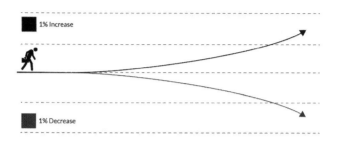

Brailsford and his coaches began by making the small adjustments you might expect from a professional cycling team. By experimenting in a wind tunnel, they found minor improvements to aerodynamics. By analyzing the mechanic's area in the team truck, they discovered that dust was accumulating on the floor, undermining bike maintenance. If one speck of dirt got into a finely tuned bike, it could degrade performance, so they painted the floor white to highlight impurities.

If you want to see the view from the top of the podium, you can't afford to get sick, not even a little bit sick, so they hired a surgeon to teach the athletes about proper hand-washing to avoid illnesses during competition. They also decided not to shake hands with other competitors during a competition to avoid contagions. They were precise about food preparation. They found the best pillows and mattresses that led to the best night's sleep for each athlete, and they brought those beds and pillows with them so the athletes could sleep in the same posture every night.

The search for small improvements created a contagious enthusiasm among the cyclists and coaches. Every team member started looking for ways to improve. As Brailford puts it, "There's something inherently rewarding about identifying marginal gains—the bonhomie is similar to a scavenger hunt. People want to identify opportunities and share them with the group."

As hundreds of small improvements accumulated, the results came faster than anyone could have imagined.

Think of it as being like the snowball effect or compounding interest—with the accumulation of daily marginal gains, you can beat anybody in the world. While everyone else was looking for the hay-maker, Brailford was focusing on the little things that may seem to make no difference, but over time, are the difference between second place and a world championship.

Urine-Soaked Insulation

Brad Harris is a shining example of how "The Aggregation of Marginal Gains" practiced over time can effect your marriage, business, or career. Like many people, Harris was told to go to school, get good grades, and get a good job with benefits. He watched his dad work the afternoon shift, 3:30 p.m. to midnight, for thirty years, then come home and take care of his family. Luckily for us, Harris' story didn't end that way.

Like Brailsford, Harris made a choice to study leadership and personal development. Through his relentless commitment and pursuit of a better life, he made distinctions and discovered core values that would serve him for years to come. Today, Harris and his wife Pam are esteemed by their peers; they are leaders in their community, sought-after speakers, and trainers who travel the world for Herbalife International.

But before all that, Harris worked as an airplane mechanic for TWA. He worked on L1011 aircraft—the largest passenger jet of its time used for international travel. What made this aircraft unique were its five restrooms in the rear. Because the aircraft had three engines, two under the wings and one above the tail, there was room for five toilets in the back. Every time an aircraft was brought in, the mechanics had to rip it all apart and replace everything, including the insulation at the rear. As Harris describes it, everyone has used the bathroom on a plane, and if you are a man, you miss half the time, so it just drains down behind the toilet and soaks into the insulation. Harris would be down in the cargo bin below the toilets, on the ramp during the summer, 115 degrees, ripping out urine-soaked insulation. For Harris, this wasn't some menial task he did for a couple of years; he foresaw it as part of his job description for the next forty years.

Like Harris, a lot of folks find themselves in the same trap. They do what is expected and get a decent job, but in the back of their minds, they really don't like their work. As an airplane mechanic, physically, Harris could take the insulation out; it's not hard to do. But it was hard for him because it was not pleasing—it was not fulfilling.

When you go into business, changing your mindset is probably one of the hardest things to do. You're not pulling out urine-soaked insulation; you're working with the toxins of your mind, and sometimes that can be harder. It only took the guy at TWA one day to teach Harris how to take the insulation out, but if Harris is going to teach you about business, he is going to teach you about mindset; he is going to teach you how to think. That wasn't taught at TWA. If you got caught thinking, you got in trouble. If Harris made a suggestion about how to do something more efficiently, TWA wasn't interested.

Accountability and Responsibility

When you are developing a business, you have to think, you have to be creative, and you have to find efficiencies. At TWA, you were not required to think; you were required to show up. Harris was accountable at TWA to punch in at 3:30 p.m. or midnight, and punch out at the end of his shift. If Harris showed up on time and clocked in, then clocked out at the end of his shift, they would never fire him.

At TWA, you were taught to work four hours for eight hours' pay. Harris was taught by his coworkers to do stuff that delayed work, like disconnecting a wire that would require an electrician to come out and fix it. At the time, it seemed like the thing to do, until one day when the electrician was delayed, so Harris and his coworkers sat and played cards for eight hours. It was a Sunday, which pays double time, so Harris was making $40 an hour. As Harris puts it, "I will never forget…I came home, and I was telling my son Tyler, who was four or five at the time, 'You should have seen Dad today. I made $40 an hour, and I didn't do anything.' Not realizing what I was saying, my son said, 'Wow, Dad, do you think when I grow up, I can get a job like that?"

Harris realized that he was setting his kid up for failure. Working eight hours with no production and getting paid for it leads to economic collapse for the company and, ultimately, unemployment for the employees. Though there were times when the team at TWA really turned it on and produced, eventually, the boredom began to weigh on him. When he first got hired at TWA, he was excited to make $20 an hour, and $40 on weekends, but eventually, all he was doing was punching a clock and waiting to punch back out. If you don't believe that, you should have been around when the horn blew to see the dead come to life and run to their cars. Harris knew there had to be something more; that's when his wife Pam found Herbalife International.

The Leadership Deficit

Harris admits he was resistant to the opportunity at first, but after losing thirty-five pounds on Herbalife International's products, his coworkers wanted to know what he was doing. Harris shared the products with his coworkers and things just took off.

Brad and Pam Harris got off to a fast start and were soon making $10,000 a month, but fast is not always good, and they didn't have the skills to maintain it. Harris, coming out of TWA as an airplane mechanic, had a job mentality, so when the income from the business started dropping, his first response was to go back and work at TWA or find another job where he could count on being paid.

In truth, the income wasn't declining because the business didn't work; it was declining because Harris' personal development wasn't matching up with his core values. Brad and Pam Harris had built a team, but they didn't know what leadership was.

According to Harris, when your income exceeds your personal development, your income will decline, no matter what. In other words, your income will always match your level of personal development and your core values. We see it all the time; professional athletes sign $20 million contracts, but if the personal development is not there, they lose it all. If they don't start developing themselves to handle $20, $30, or $40 million, it doesn't matter if they are making $150 million because when income exceeds personal development, the income is coming down.

Harris knew what family leadership was; he had watched his father for thirty years. "Just be there." That is what Harris thought leadership was. Harris' father had perfect attendance during his last ten years at TWA; his core values were, "Show up whether you like it or not," and "Take care of your family." You work forty hours a week, twenty hours of overtime on weekends, you come home to your family, and take care of your house. You are going to do all the little things yourself, like changing the oil in the car or doing the yard work. You are never going to hire anyone to do anything; you're going to do everything yourself. That's what Harris watched growing up, so that's what he thought leadership was.

On the one hand, showing up and taking care of your family is not a bad thing; however, hunkering down and doing everything himself wasn't working at $10,000 a month. And it doesn't work in a team. You can't change the oil with your team; you can't mow the grass with your team, so Harris had to start developing leadership skills.

Be, Do, Have

Harris had never been exposed to personal development. He didn't know that for things to get better, you had to get better; he didn't know any of those philosophies. Harris was around some incredible leaders who encouraged him to read the books, listen to the tapes, and attend the meetings, training, and conferences. He wanted to "have" the lifestyle, and he knew how to "do" the business—he had the "do" down. What he didn't know was the person he needed to "be" to lead a team. As a result, Harris read seventy-six books on leadership and engrossed himself in personal development.

Aware of his "leadership deficit," Harris quickly realized he needed to become someone of great value to maintain the success he and Pam had achieved. He needed to become valuable to the marketplace, valuable to people, valuable all the way around. Not only did Harris read seventy-six books on leadership, but he also committed himself to study. As Harris puts it, "I think there is a vast difference between reading and studying. People tell me all the time how fantastic the book is that they are currently reading; then they just go get another book. They never really take on the study."

There's reading, there's studying, and then there's application. Harris believes in becoming a person of great value and then teaching others the same skills. Harris knows a lot of people who have a lot of knowledge, but they don't teach. That's like being a dead sea; it's coming in and dying. The real value of your study comes from teaching. When you teach, you get feedback, and then you're able to make distinctions; that's called wisdom. With wisdom, you can start developing some core values because core values have to be from experience. Harris believes the "do" is easy; it's the "be" that requires study and time. We have to become a new creation and change our core values and beliefs if we are going to "have" success and then keep it.

Nut, Bolt, Torque

One reason Brad Harris has been so successful in business is that he understands the value of systems. As an airplane mechanic, Harris knew he could teach others to put on a bolt, put on a nut, and then torque it. According to Harris, when you are putting teams together, a football team, a baseball team, a family—when you're looking for a wife, a husband—the most important thing you do is identify their core values. Harris sees it all the time—we get really invested in someone who has a lot of skills and talent but may not share our core values.

In his book *A Path to Profits, Passion, and Purpose*, Tony Hsieh, American Internet entrepreneur and venture capitalist, shares how guiding core values played a central role in building Zappos into the mega online retail company it is today. Hsieh's company, Venture Frogs, invested in Zappos in 1999. Two months later, he became the CEO. Initially, Hsieh was skeptical about Zappos, one of the first companies to enter the online shoe and clothing space, but when he learned that footwear was a $40 billion market in the United States, and 5 percent of that was already being sold by paper mail-order catalogs, he was in. He built a system of guiding core values at Zappos, and today, it is rated one of the top three companies to work for as an employee. By 2009, revenues had reached $1 billion, and that same year, Amazon announced it would acquire Zappos for $1.2 billion.

Zappos' success attracted prominent top graduates from Harvard and Yale. According to Harris, Zappos had a list of core values guiding the company, and if the candidate's core values didn't line up with the list, Zappos wouldn't hire them. It didn't care how talented the candidate was; it wanted to know the candidate's core values. Even if the candidate were the most sought-after talent out there, Zappos wouldn't hire them. Hsieh believed so strongly in the company's guiding core values that he believed if the person had the wrong set of core values, it would eventually ruin the company.

In the mid-twentieth century, John Wooden, the coach's coach, led the men's basketball program at the University of California, Los Angeles. Nicknamed the "Wizard of Westwood," he won ten NCAA championships in twelve years as head coach at UCLA, including a record seven in a row. No other team has won more than four in a row in Division 1 college men's or women's basketball. Within this period, his teams won a record eighty-eight consecutive games.

As Brad Harris puts it, everyone wanted to know how Coach Wooden recruited athletes of such high character. Wooden would always meet with the parents and the player in the living room of their home. He, famously with his briefcase, and his assistant coach would arrive and sit down for the interview.

One of the great stories about Wooden is him walking out of an interview with the number one recruit in the nation at the time. Wooden's assistant coach lined up the meeting with the best player in the country, who was eager to join the team. All Wooden had to do was show up with his briefcase and they'd have him.

They arrived, as always, to meet with the parents and the player; in this case, the player's mother was a single parent. During the interview, the player's mother interjected something, and the player shushed her in front of Coach Wooden, telling her to be quiet. Wooden immediately picked up his briefcase, told his assistant it was time to go, and walked out. The assistant coach couldn't believe they were walking out on the top-rated recruit in the nation.

On their way back to UCLA, Wooden told his assistant that the boy had no respect for his mother, which was a guiding core value of Coach Wooden's basketball program. "If we bring that boy on our team, he'll be okay for about three practices. Then he is going to start back-talking his teammates, and then he is going to talk back to me."

Wooden, like Tony Hsieh, would always walk away from such talent, despite their skills or intelligence. John Wooden's players didn't just win championships; they were taught values and became incredible people. His leadership and mentorship transcended the game of basketball.

Brad Harris, like so many others, has found that becoming a person of great value is how you build a team. Maybe in tennis you can throw rackets at everybody and everything because you're John McEnroe, but John McEnroe doesn't have a team. You don't see John McEnroe in a doubles match because it wouldn't work. If you are going to build a team—and all of us have a team, our family is a team—when you first put it together, establish core values; then find out the core values of each individual team member.

The best way to find your team members' core values is to ask them, "What drives you crazy in other people?" The exact opposite of what drives you crazy in other people is your core value, so if people showing up late all the time drives you crazy, your core value is, "Always be on time." If you have a team around you that is late all the time, there is going to be discord.

If your core value is customer service, but the other members value getting things done quickly, there's going to be conflict.

Believe it or not, some people's core values include lying. Harris once knew a guy who was very successful in construction. This guy believed you had to lie to win contracts. In every meeting with potential clients, he would promise to start the project the following Monday, even though he knew he wouldn't be able to start for a month at least. Even when the client had a wedding coming up, and the client would ask, "Are you sure you can start the project Monday?" he would say, "Yes, Monday." The client would agree to the contract, and when Monday came, he would give the client excuses. His core value became, "It's okay to lie."

We might say we would never do that, but we might feel at times that it's okay to lie a little, right? We might pick up negative beliefs and behaviors from our coworkers; for example, it's okay to show up for a meeting in casual clothes, it's okay to show up fifteen minutes late to work, it's okay to pay your rent on the third when it is due on the first—all these subtle shifts in your core values over time affect your character.

A core value is not necessarily right or wrong, but it does make a difference. However, if we can assume that we become the composite of the five people we spend the most time with, and we put a team together that shares our core values, then that team will succeed.

Core Conflicts

When other team members' value systems do not align with your core values or the company's core values, you are working in conflict, and that creates stress, so it's important to take time to align core values with the company and the job assignment.

For example, let's say you land an executive position making $150,000 a year and part of your job is to hire and fire employees. You may believe in second chances, but now you have to let people go because the company has to deal with budget cuts. Your spouse and/or parents don't understand why you are unhappy. After all, you have a beautiful home, a beautiful car, you're making $150,000 a year—you need to step up and just be happy. This example shows why most people are in jobs that conflict with every core value of their being, and why we have a nation on Prozac. People go to a job they hate because the money is too good for them to walk away. I see that all the time while recruiting for my business.

Imagine if we considered our core values first, then the money. How many spouses are together based on their core values? If you like to travel and are leaving all the time on business trips, but your spouse wants someone who is home by their side all the time, then that relationship is not going to work. Your spouse is going to be depressed. Or, let's say "being by your spouse's side" is high on your list, but you join the military—you're going to end up divorced. Most of the time, we don't align our core values with what we do or become. If we consider our core values first, and align our core values with the company or career we choose, we will be more productive and live happier lives.

Not Right or Wrong

If we take the position that our core values are not necessarily right or wrong, but they do produce an outcome, then it is essential that we take inventory of our beliefs and core values to ensure they are aligned with our desired outcome. As 2 Corinthians 6:14 advises, "Do not be unequally yoked together with unbelievers." A yoke is a bow-shaped harness that fastens two or more animals together, especially oxen, to plow fields, move objects around, or transport goods. You can't turn the field with two oxen unequally yoked; you can't have one pulling this way and another pulling that way.

According to Brad Harris, this concept points to a critical core value we all should adopt if we want to be successful. Whether you enter into a marriage, business, job, or doubles tennis tournament, if you are unequally yoked, it's not going to work. You may not notice the issues for a year or two, but then you will suddenly realize it's not working, and you will be so overwhelmed by the fear that you are so far from where you started that you don't even want to try to get back. Maybe you are in business and have to let people go, or you're knee deep in a marriage with two kids—you can't just walk away. That's why core values are such a big deal.

We need to sit down and take inventory, identify our top ten core values, and compare them if we are going to achieve our desired outcome.

Now, sometimes you can change your core values, move them around, or develop new ones. For example, maybe you're in a marriage and your spouse wants you by their side at all times, but you need to travel for the next three years to make your business successful. If you sit down and discuss what's important to each of you, and how the business travel lines up long-term with your spouse's desires and needs, your spouse may become your biggest cheerleader. But if you don't establish that in the beginning, your spouse is going to become your biggest obstacle. Sit down to discuss core values and come to an agreement. "Let me travel for three years building the business, and then we will have the financial freedom and time we deserve to be together and live our dreams." If you don't establish this in the beginning, your spouse will fight you every step of the way.

Before going into business with someone, you want to talk with them about their core values. They may be really good at what they do, have an excellent reputation, be super-talented, and bring a lot to the table, but as Brad Harris says, "Don't fall in love with potential." A Harvard grad may be top of their class, a straight-A student, and brilliant mastermind, but if that person doesn't buy into the company's core values, they will never be a good fit. When you go into business and partner with someone or recruit new talent, identify that person's core values and ask yourself, "Do they match the company's core values?"

You will find that most people don't have an organized list of their top ten core values. The order of core values is also significant; in fact, it's one of the most important aspects of a person's value system. For example, what if one of your core values is loyalty—a good core value in business—but a candidate lists loyalty as number one and integrity as number two on their list. Loyalty over integrity is dangerous. Let's say a coworker who is friends with this person is stealing from the company; because this person believes in loyalty over integrity, they won't tell on their friend. How many people have we seen go to jail because they don't speak up when someone is cooking the books? Sometimes we need to take a look at core values and move them around. The order of core values is essential.

Designing Core Values

What Brad Harris finds interesting about highly successful people is their intentionality and their aboutness. They understand the value of a guiding set of core values and the influence these values have on their family, business, and career. Harris has designed a set of guiding core values to serve his business, marriage, and family. He keeps a list of ten core values posted above his desk, and when making life decisions or considering new goals and projects, he reviews the list, asking, "Is this going to conflict with any of my ten guiding core values?" If it does, there will be problems; there will be depression—even if the goal is accomplished, it's going to be messed up. You have to look at any new goal and ask yourself, "Is this going to match up with who I am and what I am about?" That's intentionality!

At the time of my interview with Brad Harris, the forty-first president of the United States, George H. W. Bush, passed away. During Bush's funeral procession at the National Cathedral in Washington, DC, Bret Baier of Fox News shared a letter President Bush had penned to family friend, Sam Palmisano, the former CEO of IBM. Palmisano had emailed the letter to Baier earlier in the week leading up to the procession and noted "Forty-one sent this to me in December of 2009. It says all anyone needs to know about his values." The handwritten note was the president's advice for young people.

The letter reads:

I cannot single out the one greatest challenge in my life. I have had a lot of challenges, and my advice to young people might be as follows.

1. Don't get down when your life takes a bad turn. Out of adversity comes challenge and often success.

2. Don't blame others for your setbacks.

3. When things go well, always give credit to others.

4. Don't talk all the time. Listen to your friends and mentors and learn from them.

5. Don't brag about yourself. Let others point out your virtues, your strong points.

6. Give someone else a hand. When a friend is hurting show that friend you care.

7. Nobody likes an overbearing big shot.

8. As you succeed, be kind to people. Thank those who help you along the way.

9. Don't be afraid to shed a tear when your heart is broken because a friend is hurting.

10. Say your prayers!

George Bush

Whatever your politics, I find it fitting that people of high achievement are governed by a set of guiding core values. I also find it amazing that Bush, the last president to fight in World War II, left behind these core values for young people to consider and adopt. As a product of the Greatest Generation, President Bush serves as a reminder for the youth of today of a time when personal responsibility, humility, and work ethic were expected of you. These are the guiding core values that brought our great nation out of the Great Depression, helped us fight and win a war that threatened the very fabric of our democracy, and built the greatest country the world has ever seen.

When you're young, it is hard to understand how guiding core values benefit you. One of the core values Brad Harris ranks high on his list of ten is "delayed gratification." When you go into business for yourself, you may not see the fruits of your labor right away, but I can guarantee that the core values you carry are going to dictate the outcome. If your core value is "get rich quick," you will never obtain the gratification that comes with long-term success.

Even if you achieve short-term success, it's going to slip away. Easy come easy go, right? To borrow from the promises of tomorrow, and invest yourself in the activities of today, you need to establish delayed gratification as a guiding core value, especially if you are a high producer and a type A personality, a go-getter. Because you are that type of person, you are going to imprint your core values on other people. If you have not established a guiding set of core values, there is going to be a breakdown; you are going to have stress. Guiding core values must be determined for long-term and short-term success.

Summary

The "aggregation of marginal gains" is the continuous search for a tiny margin of improvement in everything you do. With the accumulation of daily marginal gains, you can beat anybody in the world. To stay relevant in your field, you will need to acquire new skills, but it will also require changing your mindset, and sometimes that can be harder. As Brad Harris stated, "Your income will always match your level of personal development and your core values." In the Age of Disruption, companies will not only hire based on skill; they will be evaluating a candidate's character and core values. It's important to take time to align your core values with the company's guiding core values and the job assignment. Through the aggregation of marginal gains, you can become a person of great value and improve your relevance to your company or to the marketplace.

Action Steps

First, we need to become aware of our "deficit." Start by identifying some of your core values and beliefs that may be limiting your role with your company or business, then compare them with your company's set of guiding core values. In Chapter 6 of *The Relevance Gap*, I will show you how to develop your core values to align with your purpose and mission. Second, start looking for tiny margins of improvements you can make daily, and keep a list. Get your team involved and create a contagious enthusiasm to find ways to improve efficiencies and performance. Lastly, start your personal development journey and commit to reading ten pages of a good book a day, listening to audio, and attending seminars. This is where you will find inspiration and the vision you need to improve your relevance to your company, business, or marketplace.

Resources

For additional tools and training, visit TheRelevanceGap.com. To book Scott for an event or consultation, visit ScottScantlin.com. For free tips and motivation, follow him on Twitter and Facebook, and subscribe to his YouTube Channel @ScottScan1.

CHAPTER FIVE

A Different Kind of Company

"When you inspire the heart of who a person really is and attach what they are producing to a purpose greater than themselves, the product is inspiration."

— Tony Totta

In a world where all of our physical needs are met, motivation is no longer about survival. People are searching for intrinsic value; they want life to have more meaning and purpose. External motivators like a pay raise or a bonus are no longer the driving motivators—the experience is. We want to learn, grow, and be part of something greater than ourselves. Though growth cannot be imposed, we can provide an environment that understands our innate need for growth, without undermining our sense of competence.

Today with everything at our fingertips, this generation of workers, employees, entrepreneurs, and leaders is searching for meaning. They are attracted to products and companies that have a cause and serve the common good. They want to be part of something great, and they are looking to find a place where they fit into the grand scheme of a better place. They are so driven by their own personal, intrinsic motivation that they are willing to take a pay cut if it means their values line up with their search for meaning.

Engaged Companies, Inc., headquartered not far from my home in Parkville, Missouri, has a business philosophy I have come to admire. Led by CEO Chad Earwood, its motto is "People-Inspired Shipping." The company believes a person's work life and personal life should complement each other. Earwood believes that living well and working well are not opposing principles, and people of character can figure this out, find their way, and view themselves as a part of a much bigger picture—one in which they are not the center. Such people can come together in a common cause, seize the initiative, and unleash their natural inspiration and talent to do uncommon things.

Earwood believes true greatness comes when people fight through challenges and adversities, not for themselves, but to fulfill their responsibilities to others who depend on them—their family, friends, coworkers, and community. You can see it in how they act when they are not being watched. It's how they handle the roles assigned to them in any given moment. It's how they act when they are given a supporting role that is just as essential but carries far fewer accolades. These people understand that navigating one's way in the world definitely requires skill, but it also requires purpose, dedication, and faith.

Earwood says it takes a far different kind of company to recognize these people; it takes a company that hires first for attitude, character, and heart, realizing that skills can always be learned. It is a company that believes everything at home and at work begins and ends with human dignity and strives to live up to that standard every single day. It's a company that believes the journey is as important as the goal, and how you get there matters.

I had the privilege to sit down with Tony Totta, Engaged Companies' Vice President of E-Shipping, to get the backstory behind the incredible culture they have built with their employees. Before his role with Engaged Companies, Totta worked for a mid-size company selling document management software. When that company was bought by a $23 billion company out of Japan, he was branded employee number 74726.

Totta built teams for them, but ultimately, realized the company did not care about his leadership or development skills; it viewed people as property and just wanted him to manage them like company assets. His views were validated when the company went through a few mergers and acquisitions, and he witnessed people treated like property. What looked like unproductive assets in a spreadsheet affected moms and dads, wives and husbands, and community members. At the time, the Tottas were starting a family of their own. Tony remembers telling his wife that it would only be a matter of time. Eight months later, Tony was allowed to write his job description, allowing him to work three days and spend two days a week volunteering at church and spending time with his family.

In 2008, Tony Totta hosted a business luncheon downtown where he met Chad Earwood. The two men connected deeply on principles, values, business, and philosophies of human dignity. They met again and talked about the bold idea that in a world where dignity and values are often compromised, you could compete in business without compromising your values.

Earwood did not have a master business plan; he felt a call from God and walked away from a career opportunity to take over a large franchise. Being true to his heart's call, he moved from Iowa to St. Joseph, Missouri, got a business card, and started knocking on doors, knowing he had to support his family.

Three months later, a former assistant pastor came to work for Earwood. He was then responsible for another family, and that really changed things. In 2005, he began to add some franchises and agents, the model still very employee light, but he looked at that as really the launch of his company.

When Totta joined E-Shipping, he had no knowledge or background in transportation—he just knew the guy in charge was a kindred spirit, and they could build a business and see what they could do together. They changed directions and terminated the franchise agent model; Totta had a background in building a direct sales force, so he contributed that way, and then they really focused on creating a positive workplace culture. They worked on that for a couple of years, and then, what had been four guys running operations in an office about the size of a coffee shop blew up. They had a major expansion in hiring and went to ten people; however, they quickly realized the culture of this expanded business was not lining up with their values because they didn't know how to hire the right people.

That is when Earwood asked Tony to come in and run operations. Though Tony was a sales guy with no experience in operations management, Earwood offered Tony the position, reinforcing the idea that if you lead well, with purpose, you don't have to know everything about your business to do well.

Totta describes what happened next as follows:

We entered this new phase with one thought: It's all about attitude. We hung a quote by Charles Swindoll on the wall and spoke with our employees about how attitude affects the customer experience. That was the bargain we made with the team—you're going to bring your best attitude in every day; we are going to serve customers and create an excellent experience. And oh, by the way, we will learn what we are doing as we go. Our team did it, and we began to build the company together.

Today, we have more than 350 employees, and less than 5 percent have prior background in logistics. They don't come to Engaged Companies because we have a sexy industry or business model. They come because they hear something in our culture, our vision, and our mission. They understand having a purpose bigger than themselves, and we give them a practical way to engage in that. All kinds of books have been written on extrinsic and intrinsic motivation and how people are driven by both, but extrinsic motivation only goes so far, and that's what position, title, and compensation supply.

In our company, we are learning that, "When we desire something, we'll go for it, but when we find a purpose, we will sacrifice for it!" From our administrative team to our entry-level employees, we want to help the team understand the context of what they're doing every day, business-wise, but then also purpose-wise and how they fit in the mix. They're not just talking to our customers and vendors and processing shipments. Their assignment is to work accurately and efficiently, and serve well our customers and suppliers to help accomplish our mission—which is to create opportunities for individuals to fulfill their destiny in a way that glorifies God. Every shipment they process helps accomplish the mission. With every mistake, we risk losing clients, which represents losing many more dollars, so team members understand their responsibility to the vision and how they fit into the bigger picture.

It is essential that leadership is aligned with our culture and committed to our mission and values. Outside of that, the single biggest influencer is our team. Because my purpose is tied to the culture we built, I still oversee recruiting. It is easy to define culture when you only have twenty people; however, we quickly outgrew that. Today, we have two recruiters, and it is their full-time job to continually screen and recruit people.

Over the years, our most significant source of new recruits has been referrals from our employees. Good people know good people, and I tell them to refer the ones they want their paychecks to depend on because they do.

In addition to referrals, we have developed relationships with different colleges and community partners. We have one individual who sources candidates and does screening calls. Once a prospective employee clears the screening, we try to learn enough about their background to see their work ethic, define their character, spot integrity, get an idea as to whether they would fit our culture, and then if everything sounds compatible, we set up the interview. Most of the time, we use a personality study. It's not a pass-fail; it just helps us get to know people.

We are trying to figure out a few key characteristics. The first three—what skills, experience, and strengths you have—are pretty traditional interview objectives. Then we want to know who you are as a whole person. I don't believe in work-life balance; therefore, I am not going to ask you to check your life at the door and just focus on my bottom line. You're an individual, a father, a mother, a wife, a husband, a son, a daughter. If something goes wrong outside of work, it doesn't roll off your back when you walk through the doors. We want to know and understand our team so we can show them they are valued and can be real people.

Conversely, if you are getting kicked around at work and worried about covering your tail, there's negativity, and you are going to take that home. We want to reverse that spiral; we want to have an environment that sends you home every day, more alive, more human than you were when you walked through our doors. Then we work with you to identify your strengths and unleash your creative power.

We strive for clarity because clarity provides an opportunity for understanding, and understanding allows you to commit or recommit. If you commit, you can bring your passion, so we want an environment where we build each other up, where everybody works with passion, and everyone feels they are making a significant contribution. We try to gauge how you fit within and can embrace our culture. It's not perfect; it's not for everyone, but it's what we are committed to.

Once we have a qualified candidate, we find a starting point that makes sense and start our journey together.

I believe the marketplace is the last frontier where humanity depends on each other for survival. We have many options, but somewhere we have to settle into a group of people who will work together so we can get a return to pay for our lifestyle. To build that culture, Engaged Companies has developed guiding, core values we call 'The Five Es.'

The 5 Es

At Engaged, we are guided first by our values, so if you think of us as a tree, those values are our roots—they're below the ground. Everything we do is grounded in faith, family, integrity, loyalty, and maximizing human potential.

The Five Es are the tree trunk and dictate how we interact within and outside the company. They are how we integrate with each other and interact with our customers, suppliers, and community. Those Five Es are:

1. **Embody the Mission:** When you work within our company, we want you to embody our mission. But we also challenge you individually to embody your mission. You need to have a mission, you need to know what it is, and you need to incorporate it into your work life because that's the compelling cause, your purpose.

2. **Engage Beyond Yourself:** In work, what engaging beyond yourself looks like is stepping outside of your specific role. We have departments and divisions, but we don't have division lines—everybody dives for the ball, and we help each other out.

3. **Educate Yourself and Others:** Always stay hungry; always get better, and share what you learn.

4. **Evaluate Always:** Continuous improvement is our discipline. Everything we do, every call we make, every shipment we process, we need to take time—we call this the slow burn. After each task, we review what we just did, how we did it, and what we could have done better. We learn things from this evaluation that fuel not just the individual, but their colleagues.

5. **Execute Well and Timely:** At the end of the day, a good idea is a good idea, but execution wins. A good idea inexpertly executed is better than a perfect idea executed next week.

Summary

This generation of workers, employees, entrepreneurs, and leaders are searching for meaning in their work and daily lives. They are attracted to products and companies that have a cause and serve the common good. They want to be part of something that makes a difference and are even willing to take a pay cut if it means their values line up with their search for meaning. Engaged Companies is such a company and believes the journey is as important as the goal and that how you get there matters. It's a company that believes in the value of human dignity and has built a culture that supports workers' need to belong, matter, and make a difference. To stay relevant and keep up with emerging businesses that challenge the status quo, you need to provide an environment where your employees know that you care about them and the causes they believe in. When employees see an opportunity to make a difference and know that they can trust you, they will come together under a common cause and unleash their natural ability to do uncommon things.

Action Steps

What common causes, values, or mission do you serve? What is the purpose or mission of your company or business? Make a list of values that you truly believe in that best describe your company or business culture. Meet individually with your people and find out what matters to them—what are some of the common causes they believe in? Then evaluate them with your people to identify a unified cause your company serves. Then create a set of guiding core values that your people can get behind to achieve a unified mission to serve the common good.

Resources

For additional tools and training, visit TheRelevanceGap.com. To book Scott for an event or consultation, visit ScottScantlin.com. For free tips and motivation, follow him on Twitter and Facebook, and subscribe to his YouTube Channel @ScottScan1.

CHAPTER SIX

Developing Guiding Core Values

"The Universe is not punishing or blessing you. The Universe is responding to the vibrational attitude you are emanating."

— Abraham-Hicks

Frequency and Vibration

Have you ever felt like things come easily to everyone around you, while you struggle with everything you attempt to do? Most of my life, I felt set apart, not really gelling with the other kids. I participated in sports, school, and social events, but I never really felt like I fit in. As an adult, I continued to struggle with this awkward feeling of incompatibility with others. It seemed like everyone else had better opportunities, more money, more confidence, and a better sense of belonging. I just accepted the idea that I was different. I don't really understand why I felt so indifferent. In any case, I fell in with the wrong crowd, and my life went in the wrong direction for a very long time before I turned it around.

Maybe you know what I'm talking about—there seems to be a crowd of like-minded people for whom everything seems to go their way. They seem to know everyone, people go out of their way to be around them, they are successful at everything they do, and everything seems to come effortlessly to them. I wanted to know what they have that I don't.

Human beings are very complex creatures, metaphysically. Each of us has different thoughts, beliefs, values, and chosen behaviors for how we live mentally, emotionally, physically, and spiritually. The combination of these beliefs vibrating at different levels forms our overall state of being. Disempowering thoughts and emotions vibrate at a lower level frequency, while empowering thoughts and positive emotions vibrate at higher levels of frequency. In this way, the frequency we put out is attracting like-minded people to us and repelling those who do not share our current state of being.

We all run with the people we feel most accepted by—people who share our opinions, beliefs, and lifestyle. These limiting beliefs may be destructive, but they're what we know because they're the programming we came with. By default, people will impose their frequency, what they believe to be true, on others around them. If they believe something is impossible for them, then by default, they think it is impossible for us.

"If you don't change your frequency, you can't change your future."

— Scott Scantlin

If we want to change our lifestyle, we must change our frequency (thoughts, beliefs, values, behavior). This means changing our playground and playmates. When we make this radical change, we are introduced to higher level thoughts and emotions that feel uncomfortable, but we must get out of our comfort zone and learn how to adjust our frequency to pull people with more positive energy toward us.

Core Values

Core values are the source of meaning, purpose, goodness, and importance. Who are you, and what are you about? The motives and emotions behind wanting to achieve something are more important than the goal itself. Evaluating your list of core values is instrumental in changing your frequency and setting intentionality to tune in to what truly resonates with you.

As children, our parents show us the difference between right and wrong and instill in us guiding principles for living a good life. However, core values are not always positive. Our parents also inadvertently pass along their unresolved fears and doubts, and those fears and doubts get stuck in our minds for years to come.

If you grew up in a typical home, your parents or siblings most likely said things that instilled some limiting beliefs in you. Here are some common examples you may have heard around the house growing up:

- Go to school, get good grades, and get a good job.
- Money doesn't grow on trees.
- Money is the root of all evil.
- All debt is bad debt.
- The rich get richer, and the poor get poorer.
- Save it for a rainy day.

Even the best of parents unintentionally pass along their fears and doubts to their children. Once you believe something, you filter out any conflicting evidence, true or untrue, that contradicts your belief. Through the filters of your beliefs, you develop core values and narrow your attention even further to reinforce those core values. In this way, limiting core values based on fear or insecurity reinforce negative beliefs about yourself and cause you to adopt even more limiting values. Below are a few negative beliefs you may be familiar with.

- Life is hard.
- The world is a cruel place.
- You are powerless to change.
- I'm not good enough.
- I don't deserve good things.
- I don't deserve a loving relationship.
- People are wicked.
- People are unloving.

- People are untrustworthy.
- Life is meaningless.

Core values also dictate how we choose a life partner. When we are courting, we spend a lot of time exploring each other's beliefs and core values. Core values have a frequency that we either align with or we don't. If you are not equally yoked, you are going to have problems down the road. But when two people fall in love, they will often say they have the same values. However, they need to make sure their values really are the same or conflict will result down the road. Beliefs that should be investigated to ensure you are on the same page with your partner include beliefs about:

- God
- Family
- Honesty
- Trust
- Security
- Risk

Companies can also have core values. These guiding principles are often built around a core ideal and are stated in the company's mission statement. Core leadership uses these guiding principles as a beacon to keep the company on track, moving toward a common goal or purpose. These guiding principles help define how the corporation behaves in collaboration with its community and as a corporate citizen. Some examples of core values for a company include commitments to:

- building healthy communities
- innovation and excellence
- doing good for the whole
- helping those less fortunate

Imagine if we ran our lives as though we were a corporation, thinking out our core values and matching them up with our overall mission statement.

The problem with our core values is that we were not intentionally involved in forming them, so the core values currently directing our behavior and decision making may not support our intentionality. To live our dream life or move to the next level of our potential, we need to redefine and re-think our core values.

"Your philosophy creates your attitudes, which create your actions, which create your results, which create your life."

— Jeff Olson

Because so many types of core values exist, you will need to select the ones right for you or your organization. It's natural to want to create a long list of core values, so make a list of twenty more core values that best describe your organization. Narrow that down to your top ten; then choose two or three primary core values to create your mission statement. Here are some examples of core values you might choose from:

Acceptance	Common sense	Decisive	Enthusiasm
Accountability	Communication	Dedication	Equality
Adaptability	Community	Dependable	Ethical
Ambition	Compassion	Determination	Excellence
Assertiveness	Competence	Development	Fairness
Attentive	Confidence	Devotion	Family
Awareness	Connection	Dignity	Fearless
Balance	Consistency	Discipline	Focus
Boldness	Contentment	Drive	Fortitude
Bravery	Contribution	Effectiveness	Freedom
Calm	Control	Efficiency	Friendship
Candor	Conviction	Empathy	Fun
Certainty	Courage	Empower	Generosity
Charity	Courtesy	Endurance	Giving
Cleanliness	Creativity	Energy	Goodness
Commitment	Curiosity	Enjoyment	Grace

Gratitude	Love	Professionalism	Spirituality
Greatness	Loyalty	Prosperity	Spontaneous
Growth	Mastery	Purpose	Stability
Happiness	Maturity	Quality	Status
Hard Work	Meaning	Recognition	Stewardship
Health	Moderation	Respectful	Strength
Honesty	Motivation	Responsibility	Structure
Honor	Openness	Restraint	Support
Humility	Optimism	Results-Oriented	Teamwork
Improvement	Order	Reverence	Temperance
Independence	Organization	Risk	Thorough
Inquisitive	Originality	Satisfaction	Tolerance
Inspiring	Passion	Security	Toughness
Integrity	Patience	Self-Reliance	Transparency
Intelligence	Peace	Selfless	Trust
Joy	Performance	Sensitivity	Trustworthy
Justice	Persistence	Service	Truth
Kindness	Poise	Sharing	Vision
Knowledge	Potential	Significance	Winning
Leadership	Power	Simplicity	Wisdom
Learning	Present	Sincerity	
Logic	Productivity	Skillfulness	

Identifying Core Values

While some people or organizations expressly share their core values, often the best way to identify their actual values is to watch how they behave. For example, a tobacco company may be seen to emphasize profits over public health acts in a way inconsistent with a stated core value of caring for others. No company will advertise negative core values, of course, but you can judge what really lies at the heart of a business' mission by examining how it acts when it counts. A core value is only valid if it has a powerful influence and if the people or company who claim to hold it manage to live by it, at least most of the time.

As previously stated, you may have also had your core values instilled in you by your parents or community without realizing it. To get a sense of what your core values are, ask yourself:

- What activities bring me the most joy?
- What could I not live without?
- What gives my life meaning?
- What do I want to achieve?

If you can articulate those answers, you'll likely see a pattern you can boil down into a single concept, such as a consistently positive attitude or using your creativity to make the world a better place.

Core Principles

To reach for our potential and cultivate our intentionality, we have to uncover some inner truths we have developed over time and rewrite them to move us toward our imagined self. To do so, we need to evaluate our core beliefs and create values and core principles that drive us forward, and we must remove values and core principles that move us away from our desired outcome. Beliefs are very real in our mind and dictate every action. Through the process of observation, our thoughts become beliefs, beliefs become core values, and core values become core principles that reinforce our thoughts, beliefs, and values.

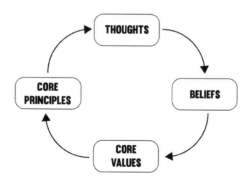

Our beliefs and core values ultimately move us toward consequences or potential. In other words, beliefs and core values directing our behavior will move us toward or away from our desires and dreams. If your core value is to play it safe, you may find yourself making excuses to justify your choices. If your core value is to take risks, when things seem impossible, you are more likely to take a chance and figure things out or find a way. Either way, your ability to engage or disengage will depend entirely on your current set of beliefs and core values.

For example, if you set a goal to become financially independent, start your own business, and leave your job in one year, but you let time pass without doing anything to reach that goal, it's possible the target may become unreachable. At the first sign that the goal may be out of reach, your mind will shift focus away from the goal and become obsessed with what's not working or what hasn't worked in the past. The experience will trigger thoughts of failure and disappointment associated with a past experience, and your beliefs and core values will direct you away from the goal altogether.

However, if you establish core values in alignment with what it would feel like to be financially independent, even though the goal has become unreachable, you can shift your focus back to the empowering emotions associated with your vision and just move the goal posts.

Recently, I attended an event where a colleague showed me a "virtual video" she had made where she had recruited top money earners in her business to congratulate her for becoming an executive director within the company as though it had already happened. They said things like, "You are awesome. Congratulations on your success. I am so proud of you. I knew you could do it. When I got the news, I was overjoyed for you and the success you have achieved." All of these statements of belief in the present moment filled her with the emotional experience of attaining her vision and goals. What was so brilliant about this virtual video was it created the experience and emotions as if the promotion had already happened. It was not limited to a time frame, so it in no way triggered emotions of frustration or disappointment—only feelings of fulfillment, pride, and joy for achieving her desired outcome.

At the same event, one of the guest speakers shared a story about his daughter, who had come across some gymnastic videos on her iPad. She was immediately fascinated and became obsessed with the videos, so much so that her father became concerned that she might "burn her eyes out" and told her to stay off the iPad.

Undeterred, she not only continued to watch the videos day and night, but she learned how to "cast" her iPad to the television as she continued with her obsession. Soon she was begging her mom and dad for some equipment, even pitching for parallel bars in the backyard. Her father found a local gym that had the necessary equipment but no real program. They did have a trainer, so her parents signed her up for classes.

At the first class, the trainer asked the parents who had previously been training their daughter in hopes of recruiting that trainer to lead a program for local youth. The funny thing was, before that time, she'd had no train-ing—all she had done was watch gymnastics videos over and over, playing them out in her mind, and imagining herself as a gymnast. She wanted to compete and would not be denied, so she recruited some friends, formed a team, and started training with the local trainer. Within a year, they enrolled in a competition.

At the competition, the speaker's daughter placed second in each event, won second in the All-Around, and consequently, was on the podium throughout the day. Her parents were so proud of her; however, in the car on the way home, they detected she was disappointed. The dad remembered his little girl had wanted a T-shirt from the event, but they had sold out quickly. To cheer up his new champion, he promised to buy her any shirt she wanted. With tears in her eyes, the daughter said, "I am not upset about the T-shirt. I am upset because I lost every competition today!"

That is an incredible insight from a nine-year-old little girl about the power of unlimited imagination and how it can transform into actual results.

She was competing more against the level of excellence she had envisioned for herself than against the other competitors. Even though she achieved second place in the state competition, meeting her self-imposed expectations was her primary goal. She could well have been the only gymnast in the gym and still have been dissatisfied if she did not perform to her expectations. What's so incredible about this story is she was competing against girls with five years of experience and finishing second when all she had was one year of training in a small town with a few teammates and limited coaching. But what she did have was vision, a strong "why," a belief in herself, and a burning desire to succeed!

"Obstacles are things a person sees when he takes his eyes off his goal."

– E. Joseph Cossman

Creating a vision for your life is the essence of intentionality. You have to take the time to define your aboutness—what you are going to be about—and then train your mind to keep the vision in the present moment. Everyone has different levels of tolerance based on their intentionality. If you are 99.99 percent committed, at some point, you will find that .01 percent reason that gives you an out, releasing you from your commitment. This is why you must choose very carefully what you are going to be about and what you are going to do about it.

"Beliefs are neither true or false, but they do create an outcome."

– Joey Klein

Bestselling author and speaker Joey Klein said creating new beliefs and core values isn't easy since you are facing your most formidable adversary—your own mind! In *The Inner Matrix*, Klein says the mind becomes aggressive when the established order changes, but if you are going to achieve your goals and dreams, you have to change your beliefs, values, and core principles. When you establish core principles that empower you, they become your new *status quo*. Think of your core principles as board members—to achieve your dreams and goals, you need to assign a board of directors that can reach your vision and goals. When you change out your board members by changing your core principles, you, in effect, redirect your behavior and actions, and ultimately, your projected outcome or vision.

Klein believes that companies today struggle to grow their business because their employees' core values and core principles are not aligned with the company's overall vision. Klein knows that until agreed-upon rules of engagement are established, employees cannot be counted on to show up on time to scheduled meetings or do the assigned homework. What he can count on is employees performing based on the current core principles. If you want to grow your business, you must train your team to align with an established set of corporate values and principles that direct the company. You can always work with employees who are struggling with job performance; what you cannot do is work with employees who have not bought into the company vision and do not understand their role in it. If an employee is not on board with your guiding core principles, you should replace them.

Whether you are running a large company or working toward personal or professional goals, you need to establish relationships that provide feedback and direction. To cultivate these relationships, you need to get plugged into an environment that supports your vision and goals. You will find like-minded people who share your passion and have the core values and principles you need to adopt at meetings, training sessions, events, seminars, and conferences.

Among your peers, you can establish relationships, find a workout partner, or join a mastermind group that will shorten your learning curve. It is vital to limit your peer group to just a few people who are trusted advisors. To narrow things even further, you need to find a mentor, someone who has achieved the success you desire and is willing to give you direction and advice.

The ultimate relationship is a benefactor, someone who does good by supporting a person or a good cause. Your benefactor is your patron, your supporter, your backer. They see value in your talents, so much so that they are willing to invest their money and time in you. When selecting a mentor or benefactor, make sure the person meets two requirements:

- They've achieved the results you seek.
- They've been able to duplicate those results.

To create core principles, you must change your beliefs to align with your desired outcome. Beliefs become core values, and core values reinforced over time become core principles. In other words, core principles are core values that have been tested over time. If your current beliefs are not producing your desired outcome, put them to the fire and challenge them—then change or modify beliefs to produce the result you want.

Summary

We all run with people we feel most accepted by—people who share our opinions, beliefs, and lifestyle. As children, our parents show us the difference between right and wrong and instill in us guiding principles for living a good life. However, the core values we inherit from family and friends are not always beneficial. Once you believe something, you filter out any conflicting evidence, true or untrue, that contradicts your belief. Through the filters of your beliefs, you develop core values and narrow your attention even further to reinforce those core values. To stay relevant, it is imperative that we become aware of thoughts, belief, and values, and evaluate whether they serve us or limit us in pursuing our potential. Once we have identified our thoughts, beliefs, and values, we can design core values and principles that will guide and direct our behavior and move us in the direction of our ultimate potential.

Action Steps

Use the list of core values in this chapter and circle at least twenty core values that best describe who you are and what is important to you. Narrow that list down to your top ten core values. Then evaluate the consequences and potential of each core value. Based on your evaluation, decide if your core values are moving toward or away from your ultimate potential. If the core value is beneficial, keep it. If not, consider core values that align with your goals. Then prioritize the list, one being most important and ten least important. If you are a part of a group or company, compare your core values to the company's guiding core values and make sure you and your team are in alignment with the company's overall mission and purpose. Make a copy of your top ten core values, post it at your office or home, and review it daily. Make it a practice to measure your decisions against your core values to confirm they align with your mission and purpose. Continually refine your core values as they are tested over time and rearrange or replace them when necessary.

Resources

For additional tools and training, visit TheRelevanceGap.com. To book Scott for an event or consultation, visit ScottScantlin.com. For free tips and motivation, follow him on Twitter and Facebook, and subscribe to his You-Tube Channel @ScottScan1.

CHAPTER SEVEN

Emotional Intelligence

"Until you make the unconscious conscious, it will direct your life, and you will call it fate."

— Carl Jung

The Epigenetic Switch

Emotional Intelligence (EI) is the ability to monitor our emotions, label them appropriately, and use emotional information to guide thinking and behavior. EI has been on and off the radar for decades. Although the term first appeared in a 1964 paper by Michael Beldoch, it gained popularity in the 1995 book *Emotional Intelligence* by author and science journalist Daniel Goleman. Goleman defined EI as the array of skills and characteristics that drive leadership performance. Today, there are many books on the topic.

Studies show that people with higher levels of EI have excellent mental health, job performance, and leadership skills. According to Goleman, EI accounts for 67 percent of the abilities deemed necessary for superior leadership performance and matters twice as much as technical expertise or IQ. Methods of developing EI have surged in the past decade. In fact, breakthrough research is now providing evidence to help identify emotional intelligence's neural mechanisms.

Have you ever done everything you were trained to do and still not gotten ahead? You were outworking everyone around you, but it still wasn't working, and you began to wonder if something was wrong with you. Kimberly and I struggled for years in our business, working fourteen-hour days, six days a week. We went to all the meetings, training, and events; made the sales calls; recruited and trained teams; took on leadership roles; read the books; listened to the tapes; and went to the seminars, but we still were not having success.

We realized a deeper issue must be going on underneath, and we needed to find out what it was. About that time, a friend introduced us to the Conscious Transformation, a body of work by bestselling author and speaker Joey Klein. The Conscious Transformation focuses on shifting core mental, emotional, and physical patterns. In his book *The Inner Matrix*, Joey Klein writes in depth on emotional intelligence and the role it plays in our daily lives. Through the work of the Conscious Transformation, we found a cutting-edge system to shift self-limiting mental, emotional, and physical patterns to a higher state of emotional intelligence that transformed our experience and removed the barriers holding us back from the success we desired.

To achieve a higher level of emotional intelligence, you must first address your epigenetics encoding. Epigenetics is the biological study of the mechanisms that switch genes on or off. Epigenomes sit on top of our DNA and alter how genes function without changing our DNA's underlying structure. Certain circumstances can cause genes to be silenced or expressed—according to Klein our "epigenetic switch" is affected by environmental triggers, including stress and trauma.

When stressful and traumatic events occur, the epigenetic switch turns on or off, increasing or decreasing the intensity with which the genes express themselves. This change ultimately affects how we choose to respond to events and challenges. Research now shows that changes in the epigenome are being passed from one generation to the next. We receive our genetic and epigenetic encoding from our parents and come preprogrammed to respond to life's challenges and opportunities based on whether or not our epigenomes are switched on or off. In other words, our genetics are the result of *the choices* made by generations before us.

Epigenetic encoding passes a multitude of information from parent to child, including emotional programming. In fact, your epigenetic switch is affected as you develop in your mother's womb. All of her fears, worries, doubts, love, hopes, and dreams during pregnancy are imprinted on your developing emotional body. When you leave the womb and experience life, the energy of your environment also affects your development. All of these factors explain why you are who you are and do what you do.

The good news is 98 percent of your epigenetic switches can be altered. Epigenetic literally means above or on top of genetics. If we can influence or change our epigenetic switch by training our emotions, we can change our destiny and the destinies of generations to come!

To effectively influence our emotions, we must reprogram our emotional responses by revisiting and redefining the meaning we attach to traumatic or stressful events. When traumatic events occur, we experience emotions like fear, anger, hatred, and anxiety. Our mind then connects these emotions to the experience to protect us from future events we identify as similar. Every time a life experience reminds us of past trauma, it triggers an emotional loop, or what I call a "trauma loop," designed to protect us from being hurt. We are transported back to a traumatic experience and relive the emotions associated with that past trauma. Although this is the mind's way of protecting us, most of the time, these emotional loops damage personal and professional relationships.

Many years ago, a good friend and mentor I held in high regard unintentionally hurt me. When I reached out to him to share my concerns and disappointment, he made light of it, and I took great offense. We didn't speak to one another for two years. Through prayer, I came to know that I needed to reconcile with him. That was the hardest phone call I ever made. When we talked, I asked him to forgive me for carrying a grudge against him. I explained what had happened, and we were both in tears. He knew I was offended, but he had no idea why. Once I explained, he was sorry as well. Our friendship is now stronger than ever.

When I did the work suggested in the Conscious Transformation, I revisited the experience through meditation to identify the emotion. Once I had isolated the emotion, as instructed, I went back farther in my childhood, to the root of the emotion, and found that I felt deeply betrayed by my father. My father, who struggled with alcoholism, left our family at a time when I needed a male role model. When he quit drinking and came home, nothing really changed. He never really explained why he left or reconciled with us. Life just picked up where it had left off. Though my father and I have a wonderful relationship today, until I looked at why I was so hurt by my mentor, I had never realized I had a deeply rooted problem with my father and had been reliving a "trauma loop" in my relationships for years.

That trauma loop cost me two years of my business. During the two years I didn't speak to my friend and mentor, I was so caught up in the emotion that I actually quit my business. I was living in reaction to a trauma loop and wanted to break the cycle. The only way to stop these destructive emotional loops from controlling you is to reprogram the event and replace the limiting emotions of fear, anger, hate, and anxiety with empowering emotions like love, excitement, encouragement, or peace.

In *The Inner Matrix*, Joey Klein says, "Emotions fuel the mind, and the mind fuels the emotion." When stress or trauma happens, emotions are attached to the event, and the mind reinforces the emotion with stories about what happened. Then we cycle or loop until we choose to break the cycle. Most people are blindly going through life directed by emotions attached to childhood events. It is like your mind is the car, and the emotions are driving. Would you allow a ten-year-old kid to get behind the wheel of your car? No. So why would you allow the emotions of a ten-year-old kid to affect the relationships and decisions you make as a mature adult?

When grown adults revisit trauma and practice methods to achieve a higher state of emotional intelligence, they quickly realize the destructive patterns of their emotions and create new associations and stories that lead to better decisions, relationships, and health.

These meditative practices have a compounding effect—the more they are practiced, the quicker you can redirect your emotions. As you attain higher states of emotional intelligence, your unconscious mind takes over and effortlessly runs your new programming. Without the weight of negative emotions, you quickly rewire your mind and your epigenetic switches. Everything feels effortless, and the limitations of your parents and generations before you no longer dictate your success or potential.

The Ninety-Second Rule

Once you become aware of how your brain functions, you can start using your brain like a computer to form your core values and core principles. Neuroanatomist and bestselling author Jill Bolte Taylor began to study severe mental illnesses because her brother suffered from one and she wanted to understand what makes the brain function the way it does. On December 10, 1996, Taylor had a stroke—a blood vessel erupted on the left side of her brain. Within four hours, she could not speak, read, walk, write, or remember anything from her past.

Her personal experience with a massive stroke at the age of thirty-seven, and her subsequent eight-year recovery, influenced her work as a scientist and speaker. She gave the first TEDTalk to go viral on the Internet. Then her book *My Stroke of Insight: A Brain Scientist's Personal Journey* became a *New York Times* bestseller and was translated into thirty languages.

In her book, Taylor gives insight into the interaction between the brain's right and left hemispheres. The right hemisphere is all about the present moment. It thinks in pictures and learns through the body's movement. Information, in the form of energy, streams in through all of our senses; then it explodes into a collage of what the present moment looks, smells, tastes, feels, and sounds like.

The left hemisphere is all about the past and future. It thinks in language and is the ongoing brain chatter that connects our inner world to our external one. Our left hemisphere is designed to take that enormous collage of information happening in the present moment, categorize it, associate it with everything we have ever learned or experienced, and project into the future all of our possibilities.

In simple terms, the left hemisphere makes sense of the present moment based on past experiences to project future possibilities. If your past experience is associated with low-level emotions and negative self-talk, your future possibilities will not be bright. However, if we change the associations of our past experiences by changing the emotions we associate with them, we can change our future possibilities.

When we experience events, a chemical reaction automatically triggers emotional programming like anger, rage, shame, guilt, and disappointment that we have stored up in our limbic system as part of our brain's fight-or-flight response from past experiences. Taylor's Ninety-Second Rule says it takes less than ninety seconds for one of these programs to trigger a chemical reaction, surge through our body, and then completely flush out of our bloodstream. However, if you retain the emotion beyond the ninety seconds, it will reinforce the emotion and become an emotional loop that will trigger automatically, affecting your decisions and future possibilities.

For example, let us say someone has disappointed you. A chemical reaction to your disappointment triggers an emotional program you call anger, which is filed away in your limbic system, designed to protect you from potential harm. Once the emotion is triggered, a chemical released by your brain surges through your body. These chemical reactions are designed to flush out of our bloodstream within ninety seconds; however, if you remain angry after the ninety seconds, it's because you have chosen to allow that emotional program to continue to run, or loop, over and over again. For most people, this is not a conscious choice—our emotions rule us and negatively affect our lives.

Once you become aware of the Ninety-Second Rule, when you feel an emotional trigger, you can decide to keep it or release it. It's like being given the keys to the vault of your mind. Instead of living in response to your emotions, through awareness, you are given a conscious choice to override the disempowering thoughts and feelings of your past experiences. You can find the Ninety-Second Rule Exercise on page 162.

Imagine that you have gotten into a blowout fight with your significant other. Your brain's left hemisphere triggers the emotional programming associated with past experiences filed away in your limbic system. As the chemical reaction begins to surge through your body, you are fully aware of what is happening and can choose at that moment to release the emotion or keep it, depending on whether or not it serves your future. As Taylor says, moment by moment, "you can choose to either hook into your neurocircuitry or move back to the present moment, allowing that reaction to melt away."

Have you ever carried a grudge and all of the emotions associated with past experiences with that person resurface every time you see them, as if the offense happened yesterday? Just the thought alone can trigger the feelings, even though the offense happened years ago. We can hold on to a grudge for years, but over time, we realize we are only hurting ourselves, and eventually, decide to let it go. By doing so, we feel a great sense of relief, as if we have been released from a great burden. That sense of relief is the chemical reaction flushing out of your bloodstream.

The good news is we don't have to wait a lifetime or even for years to release ourselves and others from emotions that disempower us. We can consciously revisit past events and reprogram our emotions by using the Ninety-Second Rule.

Without emotional reprogramming, the emotions associated with past experiences will continue to rule over decision making and future possibilities. Through a practice of Mindfulness Meditation, we can revisit past experiences and reprogram our emotional circuitry.

Mindfulness Meditation (see page 109 for a deeper dive on the subject) is the practice of bringing one's attention to whatever is happening in the present moment. Through a series of breathing techniques and meditation, you can revisit past experiences as if they were happening in the present and reprogram your emotional circuitry.

When emotions have been triggered, you have a choice to keep them or release them. In theory, emotions cannot exist without a story. If you isolate the emotion from the story, the emotion will melt away within ninety seconds. Once it has flushed out of your bloodstream, you can rewrite the story and assign new, empowering emotions that serve your future possibilities.

Emotional Reprogramming Steps:
1.   Revisit past experiences in the present moment.
2.   Trigger emotions.
3.   Isolate and release emotions.
4.   Reprogram and assign new empowering emotions.

Through Mindfulness Meditation and the Ninety-Second Rule, we can reprogram our emotional circuitry to serve us. Over time, with practice, we accumulate new references and strengthen our emotional intelligence to make sense of what is happening in the present moment and improve our future possibilities. See page 144 on the practice of emotional reprogramming.

Summary

Studies show that people with higher levels of EI have excellent mental health, job performance, and leadership skills. To stay relevant in this fast-changing world, developing the skills of shifting core mental, emotional, and physical patterns will give you a decisive advantage over your competitors. We receive our genetic and epigenetic encoding from our parents and come preprogrammed to respond to life's challenges and opportunities. When stressful and traumatic events occur, the epigenetic switch turns on or off, ultimately affecting how we respond to events and challenges. In other words, the programming of generations before us may be limiting our ability to achieve our goals and dreams. Through the practice of Mindfulness

Meditation and the Ninety-Second Rule, we can reprogram our epigenetic encoding to serve us rather than limit us in pursuit of our ultimate potential.

Action Steps

Keep a journal and note events where you feel triggered by emotions that are limiting your relationships or serve as a barrier between you and your ultimate potential. Through the practice of Mindfulness Meditation and the Ninety-Second Rule, exercise the steps illustrated in this chapter to isolate, release, and reprogram life events with new, empowering emotions that will propel you toward your inherent ultimate potential. Then repeat the process. Before long, your unconscious mind will adapt to your new programming, and you will possess the unique ability to redirect your emotions effortlessly.

Resources

For additional tools and training, visit TheRelevanceGap.com. To book Scott for an event or consultation, visit ScottScantlin.com. For free tips and motivation, follow him on Twitter and Facebook, and subscribe to his YouTube Channel @ScottScan1.

CHAPTER EIGHT

Bio-Hacking Performance

"Know the rules well, so you can break them effectively."

— The Dalai Lama

Twenty-first century scientific breakthroughs have given us the keys to unlocking boundless human potential. High achievers, the super-successful, and thought leaders around the world are obsessed with bio-hacking and bio-mining—the latest research and technology to increase performance and achieve higher human potential. Whether in sports, sales, finance, investing, technology, retail, advertising, banking, trade, marketing, insurance, or real estate, if you want to dominate your space, perform well, or just be happy with your work, you need to have intentionality about your state and physiology. Reaching your potential requires boundless energy and focus. Industry leaders, entrepreneurs, sales professional, and thought leaders are tapping into new technology to bring their ideas to market, make a better mousetrap, and increase workplace performance.

Breakthroughs in science and technology have revealed that our brains have very efficient reward systems; they release "feel-good" hormones that reward us for specific behaviors or actions. This reward system can be used to enhance learning, energize a workforce, or attract and retain customers.

For instance, corporations around the world are introducing the practice of "gamification" to increase workers' performance and creativity. Gamification focuses on instant feedback that triggers the release of dopamine, a feel-good hormone involved in reward motivation, memory, attention, and regulating body movements. By receiving virtual rewards, employees begin to associate the task and work with positive emotions, prompting them to try to repeat the experience. This same technique is used in the education system to create instant rewards for students.

Social media, marketing, advertising, and media giants have been using gamification to attract and retain customers for years. Silicon Valley refers to dopamine as the secret sauce that makes an app, game, or social platform profitable or "sticky." More than 70 percent of *Forbes Global 2000* companies said they planned to use gamification for the purposes of marketing and increased customer retention. Top executives at Facebook recently admitted that the company created "social-validation feedback loops" known as "compulsion loops" to make Facebook psychologically addictive.

You may have experienced these dopamine-driven compulsion loops personally—people around the world are glued to their phones 24/7, scrolling for the next post to get a rewarding release of dopamine. Though the use of gamification has become controversial, developers in the field of artificial intelligence (AI) are currently working on "persuasive technology" that personalizes the rewards, which should attract and retain even more customers.

Bio-hacking the human mind has become the focus of high achievers and corporations around the world. Whether developing future technology, creating a more productive workforce, increasing cognition and learning in the education system, or looking for an edge in the market, understanding the human mind and its reward systems is vital to generating the higher intentionality necessary to thrive in this new era. The good news is that you, too, can use bio-hacking techniques to cultivate intentionality and elevate your awareness, focus, and energy, helping you reach for your potential and take your business or career to a whole new level!

Getting into Flow States

"In positive psychology, a flow state, also known colloquially as being in the zone, is the mental state of operation in which a person performing an activity is fully immersed in a feeling of energized focus, full involvement, and enjoyment in the process" (Wikipedia). In essence, flow is characterized by complete absorption in what one does, and a resulting loss in one's sense of space and time.

Steven Kotler is well regarded as one of the world's leading experts on ultimate human performance. He is a *New York Times* bestseller and cofounder of the Flow Genome Project, an interdisciplinary, global organization committed to mapping the genome that lies behind human performance by 2020. In a recent interview, Kotler defined flow as, "An optimal state of consciousness where we feel our best and perform our best and moments of rapt attention, where everything else disappears into the background. Learning increases 400-500 percent during flow. You want to train your brain to operate in flow."

According to Kotler, the average person gets bored with content after two minutes and thirty-seven seconds and has the attention span of a goldfish (actually nine seconds). To compete in the twenty-first century, direct your mind away from distractions like social media and news feeds, and condition your mind to seek interests that reward you for increased focus and attention. When in flow state, you have a euphoric sense of confidence in your work, and everything seems to pour out of you effortlessly. Flow state gives you intense, prolonged focus, concentration, and energy necessary to reach your potential. Whether in sports, business, or work, when you are operating in a flow state, you are at your best. What if you could generate flow state at will? What if there were some simple steps you could take to move quickly in and out of flow? According to Kotler, flow is a four-stage cycle:

- Struggle
- Release
- Flow
- Recovery

Let's take some time now to look at each of these stages in more detail.

- In the **struggle phase**, you are inundating your brain with information. If you were a writer, this would be doing research and interviews and structuring your book. For a professional golfer, it might be practicing your swing. Training, role-playing, and presenting the features and benefits of your product might be the struggle phase for a sales professional. The struggle phase can be unpleasant and is where people with low-intentionality give up.

- In the **release phase**, you physically step away from the struggle and take your mind off the problem. You are trading slow and limited conscious processing for subconscious processing, which is extremely fast and efficient. To provide release, Kotler suggests going for long walks, gardening, building models, etc. Albert Einstein would row a boat on Lake Geneva and stare at the clouds. The ancient Chinese philosopher Lau Tsu said, "To attain knowledge, add things every day. To attain wisdom, remove things every day."

- In the **flow phase**, there is a global release of nitric oxide signaling the body to flush all of the stress hormones and replace them with feel-good hormones like dopamine, serotonin, and endorphins that underpin the flow state.

- In the **recovery phase**, on the back end of the flow state, you go from a fantastic high to an extreme low. All those feel-good chemicals have drained out of your system, and specific vitamins, sunlight, and nutrition are needed to rebuild them. The recovery stage can be very unpleasant.

If you want to get in and out of flow states, Kotler says you need to learn how to struggle better and recover better. This statement reminds me of my brother Wesley, who is the lead singer of Puddle of Mudd. Having a front row seat to Wesley's career, I saw firsthand how rock stars and entertainers were susceptible to getting hooked on all kinds of substances. You can only imagine the high Wesley feels on stage when he is in the flow state and then the crash when he leaves the stage. Staying clean and sober is a battle you will lose if you are unprepared for the kind of high you get from performing in front of screaming fans.

Flow state benefits those who practice discipline with the intent to master it. My brother saw himself being a rock star since he was twelve. He never considered any other option and spent unending hours honing his skills and mastering his art. In his book *Outliers*, Malcolm Gladwell says 10,000 hours of "deliberate practice" are needed to become world-class in any field. It may not take 10,000 hours to master your craft, but it will require an initial, unpleasant struggle. If you know what you are about, and you meditate on what you are about day and night, your subconscious mind will naturally take over, and the person you aspire to be will be integrated into everything you do.

When your skills have matured, you look for environments to test your training and compete. According to Kotler, flow state is triggered when you are deeply embodied by the work you perform in a rich environment and the consequences of your actions are high. The higher the stakes, the more intense the flow state. However, if we stay in the same role too long, we lose that heightened sense of risk needed to trigger flow and enable us to operate optimally. It's like stepping off the elevator and staying too long on the same floor. If you want to stay relevant, it is vital that you find new environments to challenge you and trigger your flow state. If what you are currently doing does not excite and scare you at the same time, you need to get back on the elevator and go to the next floor of your vision.

Win the Morning

Sadly, most of us are not skilled at generating the mental, emotional, and physical energy necessary to achieve our dreams and goals. The average person starts their day aimlessly rolling out of bed, grabbing a cup of coffee, turning on the news, checking their email and social media, and heading to a job they hate.

Interestingly, every organism on the planet has a routine it goes through daily to prepare for future stress, even species that lack a nervous system. The process through which organisms adapt for an improved response to future stress has been termed "priming." The term has also been used to describe a series of techniques and steps used by high performers to prepare for the day and get into flow state by controlling how we go about starting our day.

If you are going to be successful, you have to get your mornings right. There is a reason successful people get up earlier than everyone else—no one can bother them. Here are some steps you can follow to practice priming to own your day.

First, get up early. The more you practice priming, the earlier you will want to get up. Getting up at 4 or 5 a.m. buys you uninterrupted time to get into flow state and set your mind in motion. Between 4 and 7 a.m., you have no distractions or interruptions. The rest of the world is sleeping while you are getting focused and planning your day.

To leverage the power of daily priming, you must understand the relationship between brainwaves and our state and physiology. The mind's electrical activity is measured in frequencies. Brainwave frequencies are measured in Hertz (Hz), meaning cycles per second. There are four types of brain waves ranging from most active to least active:

- **Beta Brainwaves:** Represents a highly alert and focused mind operating at a high frequency.
- **Alpha Brainwaves:** Represents a relaxed but alert state of mind operating at a lower frequency or a meditative state.
- **Theta Brainwaves:** Represents a drowsy, sleepy state of mind operating at a slow frequency. This is the first stage of sleep, daydreaming, or indirect imagination or thinking.
- **Delta Brainwaves:** Represents deep sleep or slow-wave background thinking.

Brainwaves function at higher and lower frequencies, getting you into a rhythm that supports activities and can be useful depending on the time of day and intention.

Research has found a direct correlation between brain wave frequency and our state and physiology. When we wake up, our brain is operating in alpha state, between eight and fourteen hertz or cycles per second.

Have you ever been on your way to work and found you can't remember the last few miles you drove? Your mind slipped into alpha state, otherwise known as a daydream. Alpha state has been called the gateway to the subconscious. Writers, thought leaders, performance coaches, and high achievers know the power of the subconscious and how to use alpha state to take morning routines to a whole new level.

While in alpha state, be mindful of the signals you send your subconscious. Below are the steps you need to take daily to leverage alpha state and master the practice of priming first thing in the morning.

- **Go to Bed Early:** Priming starts the night before. High achievers understand the value of a good night's sleep. Scrolling social media, texting, checking email and news feeds, or watching TV are the worst things you can do before sleep. You want to get your mind out of beta and into theta by disengaging all beta-level activities. Thirty minutes before bed, disconnect all forms of electronics. Turn off the TV, set your mobile devices away from your nightstand, and read a book. Reading will take you to alpha state and then to theta. You will become drowsy and fall into a deep sleep.

- **Keep Electronics Out of the Bedroom:** Keep electronics out of the bedroom, including your mobile devices. Televisions, iPads, and mobile phones are a distraction; you have to condition your mind to get into alpha and theta state. When you wake up, resist the temptation to check email, news feeds, or social media. The minute you look at messages or tune into what's happening in the world, emotion enters your mind and takes over your mindset and focus. If it is absolutely necessary for you to have your phone in the bedroom, keep it out of arm's reach, on the other side of the room, away from your nightstand.

- **Don't Hit Snooze:** It may seem insignificant, but hitting the snooze button tells your brain it is okay to procrastinate. If you use your phone as an alarm clock, keeping your phone out of arm's reach, on the other side of the room, will force you to get out of the bed to turn it off. I personally have not needed an alarm for the past twenty years. When you have a purpose, your passion will wake you up every morning. The only time I need an alarm is when I am traveling and have to make a flight or be at a conference with a demanding schedule. Even then, I do not break the practice of keeping the phone away from my nightstand, out of arm's reach, forcing me to get up and avoid the temptation of hitting the snooze button.

- **Visualize:** The first twenty minutes of alpha state are critical. Before you leave the bed, make a list of goals and a list of what you are grateful for. Keep a goals/gratitude journal next to your bed on your nightstand and write down ten to fifteen thoughts that come to your mind about what you would like to happen in your life. Also, write down five to ten things you are grateful for. Meditate on your list, and visualize yourself living as if you have already accomplished your goals.

- **Clean Your Space:** Getting into a motivated state requires clarity, so you need a clean environment to work from. It is difficult to focus when your mind is distracted with dirty dishes or a messy bedroom. Doing the dishes or making your bed first thing in the morning is a small win that will train your mind to want to get things done right away. When I started on my personal development journey, I learned that if I made one change a day, given that there are 365 days in a year, I would have a 365 percent improvement in my development over a year. I was instructed to start with simple things, so I started with making my bed every day. I've been doing it every day for twenty-five years; the habit is so consistent I even make my bed when staying at a hotel. Cleaning your space sets the stage and makes you feel more organized and ready for a successful day.

- **Listen to Motivational Videos or Audios:** While you are straightening up your place and getting your environment set, listen to motivational videos and audios. Jump on YouTube where the list of motivational compilations is endless. I use a Bluetooth-enabled headset so I can listen while I straighten up my place and get ready for running and reading. If you are using YouTube, make a list and save it to your favorites.

- **Exercise:** Once I am set, I get my thirty minutes of exercise in. Exercise releases endorphins and reduces stress. Get in some cardio, go for a run, do aerobics, push-ups, sit-ups, crunches, etc. If you have a gym in your building or your home, use it. You need to get your blood pumping. Exercise is also a great form of meditation. I get some of my best ideas and visions when I am running or training my body first thing in the morning. If you belong to a gym or health club, use it, but don't let it get in the way of your priming. I belong to a group that trains twice a week for forty-five minutes at 5:30 a.m. I get up early, prime, hit the class, and get home with time to spare so I can finish priming. To get the most out of your training time, create a list of songs on YouTube or Google Play that you can listen to while you run or work out. You can also listen to your favorite podcasts or motivational videos or audio. I go so far as to write down songs or videos that catch my attention throughout the day and add them to the list. Always seek to be inspired and you will find little nuggets that drive you on and feed your potential.

- **Journal and Read:** Now that you have your goals set, you're motivated, and the endorphins are flowing, it is time to get in some reading, journaling, prayer, meditation, or writing. This is a time of *sanctuary* and the most important thing you do every day. This is when you will write out your vision or read stories about the trials and successes others have had along the way. Make sure the books you read during this time are personal development books. If you struggle with reading, listen to the books you want to read on Audible or other programs that offer audio books. You may also take this time to listen to podcasts of your favorite speakers or trainers in a specific field or discipline you want to master. If you truly want to absorb the material you are studying, I highly suggest being an active listener and taking notes. By taking notes, you create a mental file to draw from throughout the days and weeks ahead. These mental files will help you build your vision and unlock hidden potential buried deep in your mind's recesses.

- **Pray and Meditate:** Make time for prayer and meditation. Both are practices for quieting the mind, being grateful for all you have, and asking for guidance. In my prayer and meditation time, I get clarity and can see a clear plan for moving forward with my goals, dreams, and purpose. The secret to achieving all your dreams and goals is allowing a higher state of consciousness to direct you. Lastly, take time to journal or record the visions and instructions you receive during prayer or meditation. Let those quiet moments speak to your soul and give you peace, knowing what you desire will happen. If you make this a lifelong practice, you will have all the strength and direction needed to reach your potential and fulfill your purpose.

Fight, Flight, or Freeze

Recently, I was preparing to speak on a subject I had not presented on before, and I would be sharing a lot of information I was unfamiliar with. Though I was well prepared and rehearsed on this new topic, I felt nervous and questioned my ability to deliver. Over the years, I have learned that I can lower my anxiety if I reduce or eliminate uncertainty leading up to an event or presentation. Regardless of my level of certainty, when the day of the event arrives, my anxiety spikes and my hands begin to sweat.

I immediately recognized my reaction as a sign of adrenaline being released into my system. I could actually feel it coursing through my veins. I began to rehearse my presentation verbally in the car. The closer I got to the event, the more confident I became. When I arrived, my sense of awareness elevated and any sense of nervousness or lack of certainty faded away. In this heightened state of consciousness and focus, I embraced my role and performed.

The human mind has been conditioned for thousands of years to do one thing well: Identify a threat! Whether you face a wild bear about to rip you apart, see your supervisor's name on your caller ID, or have to give a presentation to your company's leadership, your brain reacts by releasing cortisol. Cortisol is the primary stress hormone produced by your adrenal glands and is designed to get you out of danger.

Cortisol, otherwise known as the "fight or flight" hormone, produces both positive and negative reactions to a threat. Regardless of your response, you will feel a surge of energy (the charge) and a heightened state of awareness (the ascent).

The first response to a threat is a release of adrenaline giving you a surge of energy. When adrenaline is pumping through your veins, your muscles become tense, you start breathing faster, and your hands sweat. At the same time, the body releases norepinephrine, waking you up into a heightened state of awareness and focus. Cortisol is also triggered, but it takes a few minutes to take effect. This natural reaction can either serve you or paralyze you, hence fight, flight, or freeze.

Cortisol and adrenaline kept our ancient ancestors alive! Stress hormones created the sudden burst of energy and speed they needed to evade wild animals. Cortisol production also gave our ancestors a heightened sense of awareness and focus when hunting. At harvest, cortisol production gave them extra energy and stamina. Although we are no longer living in caves, running from wild beasts, or hunting for survival, most of us still respond to the prospect of making that first sales call like we were trapped in a cave with a saber-toothed cat. What if we could shift away from the fear mindset and embrace the fearless mindset.

People with intentionality use fear as a motivator. They don't see threats;

they see challenges and an opportunity to grow. They do not run from a fight—they embrace it. They have become "overcomers." Not only do they embrace fear, but they also seek out situations and opportunities to feel the effects of the fight-or-flight scenario. They have developed an appetite for adrenaline, norepinephrine, and cortisol. They love the feeling of increased energy, heightened states of awareness, and intense focus. In a sense, they are engaging flow states, trusting their abilities and instincts to bring them the win.

Facing situations and events that challenge you is not only good for personal and professional growth; it is good for your health as well. These hormones only cause damage when levels stay elevated due to a malfunction in or chronic stress on your system. Elevated levels are common in our world where we deal with financial worries, family obligations, relationship troubles, and more.

Sustained elevated levels of cortisol can lead to high blood pressure, diabetes, depression, insomnia, and weight gain. *New York Times* bestselling author and "the world's leading high-performance coach," Brendon Bruchard refers to this as the "cortisol switch," where the body ceases to register the positive aspects of cortisol and switches to the negative. Cortisol feels like an energy drink; if you don't find something to engage yourself in, you crash. Unfortunately, in today's world, we are bombarded by stress triggers 24/7. With non-stop news feeds, social media compulsion loops, family obligations, and demanding work schedules, our bodies are sending inconsistent messages of counterfeit danger, which produces more and more cortisol.

People who embrace the fight-or-flight scenario receive the many benefits of a healthy level of cortisol. Occasional low levels of cortisol are expected and produce several positive effects, like regulating blood pressure, blood sugar, and insulin. These low levels aid fat, carbohydrate, and protein metabolism. When you get stressed, cortisol levels spike to give you energy and strength.

Have you ever felt nervous or anxious? When you do, you are experiencing the fight-or-flight hormone cortisol.

We have cortisol receptors all over our bodies. When cortisol is released, cortisol receptors send back a report. We express this sensation as feeling nervous or anxious. What's really happening is the cortisol receptors are confirming delivery of cortisol and the body is ready to respond.

At this point, you have three choices: fight, flight, or freeze. If you deny your body the ability to deploy cortisol properly, your cortisol receptors send back error signals, and you experience a state of increasing anxiety and stress-related health issues.

It is okay to feel nervous; you should embrace it. With intentionality, you are armed with an understanding that the feeling you are experiencing is the body's reaction to stress. With this understanding, you can harness the power of cortisol. By realizing we are no longer living in caves and the physical threat is non-existent, we can make new choices and embrace the benefits of stress hormones. So, the next time you are staring down that phone and about to make your first sales call, make the switch and embrace the experience.

Because it has become known as the "stress hormone," cortisol has gotten a bad rap. I think it should be renamed the "success hormone" for the role it plays in giving us the energy, focus, and strength we need most when facing life's greatest challenges.

Nootropics: The Holy Grail of Mental Focus

Another successful bio-hack was the discovery of nootropics. Also known as smart drugs and cognitive enhancers, nootropics are supplements and other substances that improve cognitive function, mainly executive functions, memory, creativity, or motivation in healthy individuals.

My fascination with supplements that could enhance brain performance and capacity started when I watched the movie *Limitless* starring Bradley Cooper. The film follows Edward Morra, a struggling writer introduced to a nootropic drug called NZT-48, which gives him the ability to fully use his brain and vastly improves his lifestyle.

In my search for the Holy Grail of mental focus and peak performance states, I was introduced to nootropics through a Netflix Original documentary *Take Your Pills*, about the abuse of Adderall, an amphetamine with a chemical makeup similar to methamphetamine. Once Adderall gets to the brain, it mimics the actions of the neurotransmitters epinephrine, norepinephrine, and dopamine, although in higher quantities. The film features college students who use it to study harder, a guy in finance who takes it to work longer hours and make more money, and a music agent who says it gives him more pep and the ability to deal with clients. Adderall is used to treat ADHD (attention-deficit/hyperactivity disorder); however, it is also used by athletes to enhance performance, students to improve cognitive function, and professionals to work longer, more productive hours. It is even used as an aphrodisiac and euphoriant.

Like the fictional drug NZT-48 in *Limitless*, Adderall has side effects and addictive properties; it can lead to dependency and cause irreparable harm to those who abuse it. Although the documentary highlights how widespread Adderall abuse is, it is more about the pressure people are under to perform and how far they will go to compete.

In *Take Your Pills*, Alternascript, a California-based company, offers an alternative called "Optimind," with an all-natural nootropic supplement to boost brain performance and cognitive function. Optimind is used by professionals, students, athletes, and gamers for the increased focus and concentration needed to work smarter, work longer, and get the job done.

When Kimberly and I were in our late forties, we were struggling to sustain focus and concentration on projects. When I used a sample of Optimind, I saw immediate results. Then I started Kim on the supplement. The results have been outstanding. We are experiencing the sustained energy, concentration, and focus we need to complete tasks, as well as the increased cognitive function and memory necessary to keep up with the demands of today's fast-paced society.

Mindfulness Meditation: Training the Mind

In our fast-paced society, with everything coming at us 24/7, our minds are racing from thought to thought, through a never-ending cycle of news feeds, social media posts, work, and our personal lives. It seems almost impossible to string together a few seconds of focused attention, let alone twenty minutes. However, these twenty minutes of focused attention are the key to strengthening our ability to sustain concentration, which is key to achieving intentionality.

The practice of Mindfulness Meditation, which has been used for centuries, has become the most beneficial form of meditation in modern society. Twenty minutes of mindful meditation a day helps overcome the impulse to react to everything we experience throughout the day and take control of our thoughts and mental focus. In addition to increased mental focus and a sustained level of concentration, mindful meditation also yields the following health benefits:

- Reduces stress
- Controls anxiety
- Promotes emotional health
- Enhances self-awareness
- Lengthens attention span
- May reduce age-related memory loss
- Can generate kindness
- May help fight addictions

As a practitioner of Mindfulness Meditation, I can tell you it is difficult to do at first. You are asked to still your mind and focus on a single thought for twenty minutes. As you can imagine, your well-conditioned mind will be racing with thoughts, but the goal is to concentrate on a single thought for twenty minutes, keeping your mind fixed on the present moment. As your mind strays, you must quickly recognize your thought and turn your attention back to focusing on it. This is done by focusing on the four-sided breath or "box breathing," a breathing exercise that calms the nervous system and keeps you anchored to the present moment.

In box breathing, you touch your tongue to the roof of your mouth to engage the vagus nerve, then expel all of the air from your chest. Keep your lungs empty for a four count. Then inhale through your nose for a four count. Breathe in gently as though you are trying not to disturb a feather below your nose. Hold the air in your lungs for a four count. When you hold your breath, do not apply pressure; rather, try to maintain a relaxed feeling. When ready, release and exhale smoothly through your nose for a four count. This is one circuit of box-breathing. Repeat the process, and keep your focus on your four-sided breath.

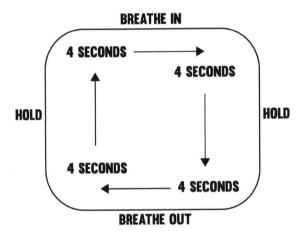

It sounds ridiculous, but this method is used by Navy SEALs and snipers to maintain focus and concentration. This method of Mindfulness Meditation has attracted a growing number of scientists eager to learn more about meditation's cognitive effects. In fact, researchers at UCLA have found that long-term practitioners of meditation have significantly more "gyrification" or "folding" of the cortex, which may allow the brain to process information faster. Furthermore, a direct correlation was found between gyrification and the number of years the practitioner meditates, possibly leading to more proof of the brain's neuroplasticity or ability to adapt and change to the environment.

I know it seems simple, but meditation is hard work and requires a daily commitment. For the practice to be effective, find a comfortable spot to meditate and schedule your twenty minutes daily. This should be a space where you are not easily interrupted, like your personal office, a spare bedroom, or even your closet. For example, I meditate in the mornings in our spare bedroom, or at two-thirty in the afternoon at my office. You may need to inform others not to disturb you during your scheduled time. I would also suggest using a guided meditation—you can find many on YouTube or subscribe to a service like Conscious Transformation with Joey Klein for deeper meditation and coaching.

Repetition is the key to meditation—the more you do it, the easier it becomes. As a matter of fact, you will find your subconscious mind, over time, will begin to implement the techniques you practice during meditation, bringing peace and success to the opportunities and challenges you face throughout your day.

Summary

Bio-hacking the human mind has become the focus of high achievers and corporations around the world. Whether developing future technology, creating a more productive workforce, influencing behavior, or looking for a decisive advantage in the market, understanding the human mind and its reward systems is vital. To stay relevant and compete in a performance-based economy, use bio-hacking techniques to elevate your awareness, focus, and energy, helping you reach your ultimate potential and take your business or career to a whole new level.

Action Steps

Make a list and identify some areas where you are lacking and could benefit from adopting some of these habits and principles. Next, skim back through this chapter and highlight some of the techniques you would like to implement to improve your performance. Then take small, daily actions to integrate these techniques and habits into your daily routine. Before long, those simple 1 percent improvements will create radical, transformational change and give you the energy, focus, and patience necessary to stay relevant in your career and business.

Resources

For additional tools and training, visit TheRelevanceGap.com. To book Scott for an event or consultation, visit ScottScantlin.com. For free tips and motivation, follow him on Twitter and Facebook, and subscribe to his You-Tube Channel @ScottScan1.

CHAPTER NINE

The Power of Mindset

"Whatever the mind can conceive and believe, the mind can achieve."

— Napoleon Hill

To condition the intentionality of our minds, we must first recognize that our minds have been conditioned for thousands of years. Much like a computer, our minds come preprogrammed with software designed to protect us. If we allow our minds to run as they are preprogrammed, we are destined to repeat the lives of generations before us. Romans 12:2 says, "Do not conform to the pattern of this world but be transformed by the constant renewing of your mind." If we never take ownership of our mind, it will rule over our thoughts, beliefs, and emotions. By applying what you learn in this book, you are using emotional intelligence and Mindfulness Meditation to reprogram your epigenetic encoding and rewrite your destiny.

Think and Grow Rich by Napoleon Hill is one of the greatest books ever written on success. In 1908, Andrew Carnegie commissioned Hill to meet with the wealthiest men in the world and identify the characteristics they share and the secrets to their success. Hill published the book in 1937, and it had sold 20 million copies by his death in 1970.

Hill believed your mind was your greatest ally and your greatest enemy.

He suggested it has the power to attract emotions that arise from deep within one's beliefs and faith. Therefore, if you have faith in a desire and believe it will come true, it will begin manifesting into its physical self. Hill goes on to suggest that the mind will manifest our existing beliefs, even self-limiting beliefs. Hill believed our beliefs hold so much power that they almost always come true, even when they are self-sabotaging. Therefore, if you want your desires to become reality, you must develop your intentionality, or mindset, to believe in what you desire and have faith that it will come to you.

Hill also believed our thoughts are, in fact, real. In the very first chapter of his book, he says, "Truly, thoughts are things, and powerful things at that, when they are mixed with definiteness of purpose, persistence, and a burning desire for their translation into riches or other material objects."

If the content of our thoughts—the desired, the believed—are in fact real, as argued by Hill, then we should learn to harness the power of our mind to produce the desired and the believed of our choosing. In the chapters ahead, I will show you how to harness all of your resources and understanding to develop the intentionality, or mindset, that will help you reach your potential and achieve dreams beyond your wildest imagination.

To achieve your goals, you must learn to recognize failure as part of the process. People with highly developed intentionality recognize failure as data or feedback. They know goals are realized by sustained activity over time, and failed attempts are necessary so they can make distinctions. With the *feedback of failure*, we can make adjustments, moving us ever closer to realizing a goal or vision. People who lack intentionality perceive failure as a threat or as painful. They experience fear and develop approach-avoidance. Even with the best of intentions, their preprogrammed minds work against them. To succeed, you need to reprogram your thoughts, feelings, and emotions to recognized setbacks as evidence that you are making progress toward your goals.

People with developed intentionality do not react to what is happening on the surface of things; their focus is fixed on the horizon. They do not allow temporary setbacks to interrupt their aboutness; they stay focused and trust their mind will sort out the details that need to be addressed three feet in front of them. Their boundless energy and relentless pursuit of vision are supported by faith and the belief that they are unique and have all the resources necessary to achieve their desired goals.

Break Away from the Herd

I have spent years in the personal development and business space, and the single biggest mistake I made was standing in someone else's shadow too long. "Mentors are put into your life for a reason, but only for a season." There comes a time when you have to break away from your instructor and spread your wings. Living in someone else's shadow subjects you to their limitations. Don't misunderstand me. You are going to need mentors, trainers, and teachers along the way, but don't stay too long. You only need to spend so much time with each one—then you have to break away if you want to reach your potential!

To break away from the herd, you also have to break away from average people. That means limiting time with friends and family who are not in alignment with your vision and goals. Average people don't like it when someone strays from the herd. They are going to tell you things like "You can't do it," "You'll never make it," or "It's a scam." By chasing after your dreams, you're reminding them of the dreams they gave up on and how they settled for ordinary. The truth is they don't want to be left behind, left alone, or left on their level.

I recently attended a three-day transformation weekend seminar where the trainer routinely asked for feedback. The second day, a woman shared how her husband had torn into her when she got home the previous evening. He was afraid she was going to leave him if she continued with the program and started to change. She almost didn't come back.

The Law of Association

The Law of Association says you are the average of the five people you spend the most time with. If you're hanging around your four broke friends, you're bound to be the fifth one. Much like the Law of Attraction, the Law of Association is based on the frequency of our emotions and experience.

Frequency is the rate of vibration and oscillation of our mind's electromagnetic activity. When we reach a high-level frequency, we attract more positive emotions into our experience. Love, for instance, is a very high-frequency emotion. When we emit a low-level frequency, we attract negativity, stress, anxiety, and depression.

Much like Wi-Fi on electronic devices, our minds are preprogrammed to connect with the frequency of the people around us. Not only does our mind seek to connect, by default, but our mind will mirror the thoughts, beliefs, values, and behaviors of the people we spend the most time with. Even those with strong opinions and viewpoints will find themselves drifting away from their values when exposed to low-frequency emotions if their intentionality is not well conditioned.

The best way to determine if the people in your environment are holding you back is to ask yourself these four questions:

- Who am I around?
- What are they doing?
- How is it affecting me?
- Is that okay?

To have the right intentionality, you have to decide if the company you keep is helping or hurting you. Are these people celebrating your success and cheering you on, or are they doubting your every move and holding you back? Are they running in the same direction as you, or are they settling for average? Know this: If you buy their opinion, you buy their lifestyle.

Success requires changing your playmates and playgrounds. That may mean leaving some people behind. To help you decide on how your associations are formed, follow the Law of Association and its counterparts:

Law of Association: Your goal is to form associations with people operating at a higher-frequency than you and who have the lifestyle you want—people moving in the direction of your goals whom you need to connect with to achieve the lifestyle or dreams you are pursuing. By changing your playmates and playgrounds, you change your frequency, and your mind, by default, will begin to adopt the thoughts, beliefs, values, and behavior of your new associates.

Law of Limited Association: You may need to limit your exposure to extended family members or loved ones who have firmly held opinions, beliefs, and expectations not in sync with yours while maintaining your relationships with them. By default, family has so much influence over your life that you may unwittingly subject yourself to their overpowering beliefs or low-frequency emotions. You will need to set boundaries with your family if you want to achieve your goals.

By setting boundaries, we set our expectations, as opposed to being subjected to someone else's expectations. Family tends to compel you to consider their needs or expects you to assist them in solving their problems. Limiting time while maintaining relationships means not solving other people's problems while continuing to participate in family events and holidays.

It is also essential to set boundaries with your spouse and children when you are working at home. You need to set expectations and patterns that allow them to know when you are available and when you are not. Your spouse and children have expectations as well, so make sure you understand and meet them, setting and guarding family time. Then do not violate it. They will support you and buy into your vision when they clearly see your expectations and that you also take their hopes and expectations seriously.

Law of Disassociation: This law refers to people you need to leave behind. They are friends and coworkers who always operate in low-frequency emotions. They may be good people, but are not suitable for you. They are not goal-oriented and have no desire to pursue their dreams. They see change as a threat and have settled for the status quo. Their goal is to maintain the lifestyle they have and protect it at all cost. They spend their lives comparing themselves to others on social media and focusing on major or minor things they have no influence over, like politics or what happened on The Bachelor last night. They have no desire to change and will most likely push back when you do.

I believe we have the potential to affect people and places around us. However, do not underestimate the power of low-frequency emotion. If our intentionality is not secure, if our faith is not fixed, we will be overpowered by our environment. If we want to have an effect on the world around us, we must first look inwardly at our own intentionality so we can stand firm in the face of adversity when we break away from low-frequency mindsets.

When you break away from the low-level frequency, it's kind of like kicking a beehive—it may sting a bit. Average people's low-frequency emotions are conditioned to recognize change as a threat; however, if we continuously monitor our environment and use the Laws of Association, Limited Association, and Disassociation to guide us, we can strengthen our intentionality, and eventually, break away from the self-limiting beliefs we've adopted from other people.

We change the world when we learn to operate in higher-level emotions and hold space for others. We must first hold space for ourselves before we can hold space for anyone else. Practicing the Laws of Association will provide the space you need to develop and grow your intentionality so you can use your gifts to create and hold space in the world around you.

Summary

According to Napoleon Hill, your mind is your greatest ally and your greatest enemy. Hill believed our beliefs hold so much power that they almost always come true, even when they are self-sabotaging. If "Thoughts are Things" as stated by Hill, and powerful things at that, then it is imperative that we develop the skill of taking our thoughts captive so we can shape our destiny. We are all products of our environment, staying relevant in our career and business requires constant evaluation of our relationships and how they affect us.

By evaluating your relationships, you can consciously choose associations that move you toward your ultimate potential, disassociate with people who are holding you back, set boundaries with friends and family who may be limiting your growth, and set expectations with the people you love and care about most. Through repetition, you can harness the power of your mind to shape your destiny and reach your ultimate potential.

Action Steps

Now that you understand the Law of Association, list the five people you spend the most time with. Review each relationship and decide if the association is moving you toward or away from your ultimate potential.

1. _____
2. _____
3. _____
4. _____
5. _____

Which people do you need to limit associating with?

1. _____
2. _____
3. _____

Identify three people you would like to associate with who can help you get closer to achieving your goals.

1. _____
2. _____
3. _____

What things can you do to begin associating with these people or how might you contact them? Be specific, such as, "Ask Pat out for coffee."

_____
_____

TIP: You may need to level up your value to become worthy of their attention. The best way to become the person of value that they associate with is to read books, listen to audio, and attend conferences that they support. Become a volunteer and be available.

You will be surprised how quickly you are pulled into the associations that will elevate you to your ultimate potential and the person you desire to be!

Resources

For additional tools and training, visit TheRelevanceGap.com. To book Scott for an event or consultation, visit ScottScantlin.com. For free tips and motivation, follow him on Twitter and Facebook, and subscribe to his YouTube Channel @ScottScan1.

CHAPTER TEN

Cultivating Clarity

"The first law of success is concentration—to bend all the energies to one point, and to go directly to that point, looking neither to the right or to the left."

— William Mathews

To develop your intentionality, you need to clearly define the gap between where you are and where you could be. This requires a process of several steps, not necessarily in a certain order, that we will investigate here. Those steps are:

1. Get Clarity
2. Consolidate Energy
3. Raise Necessity
4. Be Willing to Starve a Little

Get Clarity: Successful people are never satisfied with the status quo; they understand the value of slowing down to speed up. They take time to take inventory of their current model, ask questions, and consider new methods and possibilities. They consider their value proposition and delivery systems. They look at the experiences others are having in similar industries and take into consideration how changes affect their business model.

Successful businesses get absolutely clear about their situation and where their focus should be. To evaluate your business, ask yourself these questions:

- Has my value proposition changed?
- Have the characteristics of the market changed?
- Am I using current marketing methods to generate new business?
- Is my business "sticky"? Am I retaining repeat customers and clients?
- Am I attracting the customers and clients I want?
- What sector of my business or industry is having the most success?
- Am I out front? Do people know me?
- Are my current responsibilities holding me back?
- Am I efficient?
- Are my team players operating in efficiency?

Once you have a clear understanding of where you are in the scheme of things, you can develop a clear vision of where you could be and the change required to get there. The next step is to consolidate energy by identifying the two or three things that will produce results and move you toward your potential.

To attain this clarity, we will use the Pareto principle. The Pareto principle was developed by Joseph Juran and is based on the work of eighteenth-century Italian economist Vilfredo Pareto. The Pareto principle, otherwise known as the 80/20 rule, states that roughly 80 percent of effects come from 20 percent of causes.

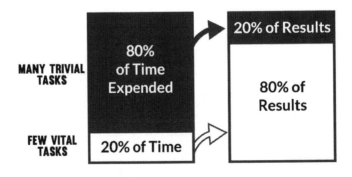

Pareto diagrams are based on the principle of separating vital tasks from trivial tasks.

What if everyone on your team had a vision of their own intentionality and the company's overall potential? What would your business look like if everyone on your team knew they had a stake in the outcome? It is absolutely essential that your organization is crystal clear about the importance of the tasks each individual performs and what their stake in the outcome is if you want your business to go to the next level.

I was recently working with Troy, a good friend of mine who owns a small jewelry shop in Parkville, Missouri. Troy was struggling with keeping and motivating his employees. When he found good employees, they would only stay with him for a short time, and keeping them engaged with daily tasks was a constant challenge.

Being familiar with his business, I knew Troy's employees were not there for the money. His company was a boutique shop in historic downtown Parkville, operating out of 800 square feet. He only has two or three employees at any given time, and they are standing on top of each other most of the time. Troy is a master jeweler, otherwise known as a *bench jeweler*. People come to work for him because they want to learn the trade.

It was clear to me that Troy was attracting the right people; they just lacked a clearly defined vision and had no stake in the outcome. I suggested Troy take an apprenticeship approach with his employees with a promise of developing their skills over two years.

Troy had also wanted to expand his shop into a bigger facility, so I encouraged him to do so and include his team in creating a vision for the new establishment. With his new place, he could showcase his workshop and his apprenticeship program, while providing the personal touch you can only get from a local jeweler.

When your employees understand the value proposition and have a stake in the outcome, they engage in the process—turn your employees into *stakeholders*.

Consolidate Energy: Everyone on the team should know their role. The fact is, we spend most of our time bogged down with menial tasks and lose sight of the two or three things that actually produced results and grew the business. What if everyone on the team were absolutely clear about the company's direction and had clearly defined tasks based on the two or three things they do best—things that actually produced results and grew the business?

In *Eat That Frog*, Brian Tracy describes the law of forced efficiency as follows: There is never enough time to do everything, but there is always enough time to do the most important thing.

In a given day, we do fifteen to twenty things, most of which produce no real results. When our team is absolutely clear about how the two or three things they do produce 80 percent of the results, you force efficiency and grow the business.

Raise Necessity: Consider what's required and be willing to do it to achieve your goal. Requirements may include a short-term setback to adjust your focus. They may also require new skills and systems to be put in place. On the other hand, you may have a model that is working well, but you need to recruit new talent to grow within your current model. You may need to invest in marketing, product development, or delivery processes to move to a higher level of production and reach your potential. I was recently researching a company that registered for one of our luncheon events. The company president said in a video on their website, "Hiring the right people isn't a priority; it's a must!"

Successful people get absolutely clear about what is required to achieve the next level of potential. In their eyes, the consequences of inaction are unacceptable. They meditate on the vision day and night and work tirelessly toward fulfilling the well-defined requirements. They know the value of failure and understand that without all-out, massive action, there will be no victory. They are clear about the requirements and have narrowed their focus down to the two or three things that will produce the desired results. Everyone on the team has bought in and has a stake in the outcome. When the promise of achieving new levels of potential is higher than the requirements for achievement, work is effortless.

Be Willing to Starve a Little: Successful people know the value of going hungry. Hunger is a requirement if you want to develop your intentionality. I have always performed best when my back's against the wall and I'm a little hungry. When I am starving hungry, I am unstoppable!

I am not suggesting starving yourself. What I am suggesting is getting away from the trappings of your success. When all your needs are met, you become a docile creature of habit. Like caged lions at the zoo with meals at dawn, you lose your innate instincts to hunt. You need to find your hunger and wake up your intentionality. When you are chasing the next level of potential, you can simulate hunger and trigger instinct by temporarily stripping yourself of your success' trappings and comforts. The practice of fasting in many religions around the world produces this effect. By denying yourself the pleasures of your current lifestyle, you trigger instinct and wake up the lion inside of you.

In the movie *Rocky III*, written and directed by Sylvester Stallone, former working-class boxer Rocky Balboa has become the world heavyweight champion. However, his fame and wealth have made him lazy and overconfident. His number-one contender, Clubber Lang, accuses Rocky of intentionally accepting challenges from lesser opponents to avoid fighting him. Rocky's trainer, Mickey, confesses that he handpicked the opponents for Rocky's title defenses. Mickey explains that Lang is young and powerful, and most of all, "hungry," and that Rocky won't last three rounds because he's lost his edge and become "civilized." In a double whammy, Rocky loses his trainer and father figure when Mickey unexpectedly dies, and then he loses his title to the challenger, Clubber Lang. Turning to his former adversary, Apollo Creed, for help, Rocky struggles to get his old fire back. Apollo takes Rocky away from his trappings of success to the streets of Los Angeles to train in the gym where Apollo once trained. There, Rocky finds his fire, making him able to defeat the arrogant Clubber Lang and regain his title.

Have you lost your fire? Are you hungry, or are you satisfied with being civilized? Are you willing to do what is required to get that fire back? It may require stepping away from titles, the trappings of success, and the comfort of home and family, but it will be worth it.

Recently, I have been working on a project that will dominate an entire sector of my business and take my team several levels beyond the next level of potential. This project requires implementing a new strategy and new marketing methods. Once I realized the project's potential, I had the energy to work tirelessly day and night to achieve my goal. I also got buy-in from team members who shared the vision and wanted a stake in the outcome. The closer I got to the goal, the more focused I became. The project required some talents and skills I did not have, so I recruited those talents in house and used freelancers for any missing components. We did some test launches and got the results we were looking for.

At that point, I became restless. Like a starving lion with one mission, I began to pace the floor, demanding intense, focused action from my team and from myself. And there it was—hunger driving me! I wanted to make a kill; I wanted to close a new account with our new system. I got so excited about the possibility and wanted to be running at capacity within thirty to sixty days. This is the power of potential, the power of realizing a new level of accomplishment. This is what you are designed to do. Realizing the potential of an idea or well thought out plan you have meditated on, labored on, starved for, and sacrificed for is a driving force like no other. You become unstoppable. It has all the elements of a flow state: deep embodiment of the work, productive environment, and high stakes. Nothing is more rewarding than the realization of a worthy idea.

Summary

We spend most of our time bogged down with menial tasks and lose sight of the two or three things that actually produce results and grow the business. Successful businesses get absolutely clear about their situation and where their focus should be. To stay relevant and compete in the marketplace, you need to become absolutely clear about where you are, and where you could be, and narrow your focus down to the two or three things that produce results and move you in the direction of your ultimate potential.

Action Steps

Meet with your team and make a list of everything they do during the work week. Find out what's most important to them, and become absolutely clear about the two or three things on the list that line up with who they are at heart and that produce results. Then help them delegate and prioritize all other supporting activity so they are performing the tasks that produce results during your business' peak hours. For sales professionals and entrepreneurs, repeat the process. Identify the two or three things that produce results; then schedule supporting activity to be done during non-peak hours so you can perform tasks that produce results during your business' peak hours. If you are in sales and marketing, your business depends on a strict observation of the 80/20 rule.

Resources

For additional tools and training, visit TheRelevanceGap.com. To book Scott for an event or consultation, visit ScottScantlin.com. For free tips and motivation, follow him on Twitter and Facebook, and subscribe to his You-Tube Channel @ScottScan1

CHAPTER ELEVEN

Creating a Vision

"The best way to predict the future is to invent it."

— Alan Kay

The key to understanding the power of vision is knowing who you are, what you are about, and adopting a mindset for success. To do this, you need to:

- Create a vision for your life
- Clearly define your goals
- Adopt a mindset to achieve it

Like many of my entrepreneurial friends, my mother was a visionary. She was always reading books, listening to tapes, and going to seminars. Luckily for me, she introduced me to the world of personal development in my early twenties when she gave me a copy of Tony Robbins' audio series *Personal Power*. I listened to it in its entirety and did the work.

Robbins suggests we set crazy, unrealistic goals, beyond our wildest imagination. I set one-year, five-year, ten-year, and twenty-year goals. I did the visualization technique, planting the vision deep in my subconscious mind and anchoring it into my nervous system. I created a vision for my life that included one day becoming a bestselling author and keynote speaker, traveling the world with my wife, and having a boat and a plane that would allow us to help families in poor countries. I wanted to become an actor and even write and direct movies. All of these crazy, unreachable dreams were put in writing when I was a broke, twenty-five-year-old failure living in his mother's basement.

Over the last twenty years, I have lived out the vision I set for myself in my early twenties. I married a fiery redheaded Christian girl (as it was explicitly written in my vision). Though we have no children of our own (yet), we are supporters of the Global Orphan Project, serving orphan children in Haiti and around the world. With this book, I am working toward my goal of becoming a bestselling author and successful keynote speaker. We own multiple businesses that provide a lifestyle that most only dream about. Kimberly and I travel the world together doing what we love and helping others to achieve their dreams and goals. We are living proof that anything is possible—all you need is a vision, clearly defined goals, and the intentionality to get there.

To achieve our goals, we need to make a distinction between our vision and our goals. Vision is where we see ourselves in the future, our ideal self. Vision has no boundaries, no expectations or limitations. *Vision has no finish line!* Vision is not subject to the emotions of frustration, anger, or disappointment. Vision is the thing you long for when you grow tired of what you are doing. You innately think about it unconsciously day and night. Part of life is about discovering why you are here. Who are you? What are you about? To create a vision for your life, you need to take inventory of your skills, talents, experience, and history. Answer these questions:

- What are you good at?
- What are you passionate about?
- What do you naturally do better than anyone else?
- What are your strongly held opinions?
- What's most important to you?

To create a vision, you have to know where you are going and what it looks like, and you must commit to what will be required until the vision is fulfilled. When developing your vision, you want to start with the end in mind; what is your desired outcome or the end result you want to experience? The very thought of your vision should inspire you. Your vision should get you up early in the morning and keep you up late at night. Your vision should serve as the compass you look to over and over again to evaluate if you are moving toward your vision or away from it.

Joey Klein, author of *The Inner Matrix* and founder of Conscious Transformation, says, "Vision is more important than goals." We often confuse vision with goals. When we fall short of our goals, frustration and disappointment shift our focus away from our vision to what's not working or what's not gone well in the past. I'm not saying goals are not part of the process, but when you confuse vision with goals, you set yourself up for disappointment. Having a clear, well-defined vision will allow you to continue on course and adjust your goals along the way. When you shift focus away from vision to what's not working, go back to your vision and let it fix the problem.

Grant Cardone says, "You should have a vision so big that your problems pale in comparison." Vision is the North Star that guides you. It allows you to make changes and adjust your goals on the way to your destination. Goals are the benchmarks that need to be accomplished to move you to the next level when making your ascent and reaching for your vision.

When we make the distinction between a *vision* and *goals*, we can use short-term and long-term goals as milestones moving in the direction of our vision.

What kind of impact do you want to have on the world? If you can develop a clearly defined vision in line with your own personal values, you will be drawn into it. You already have everything you need inside of you; all you need to do is develop your vision and start your ascent.

Clearly Defined Goals

It has been said that goal setting is the gateway to your dreams. I have long been a huge fan of setting goals. For goals to be realized, they need to have some specific qualities and characteristics. Having good intentions without clearly written goals and an action plan to achieve them is just wishful thinking. To be an effective goal setter, you should use the following six rules of goal setting, which I have used for more than a decade. Your goals must be:

1. Written down
2. Specific—clearly defined
3. Have a timeline—set a deadline
4. Have a plan
5. Something you're willing to pay the price to achieve
6. Verbalized—say them

Let's look at each of these requirements in more detail.

1. **Write It Down:** Goals must be written. Whether you want to lose weight or earn six figures in the coming year, writing out your goals on paper and reviewing them daily trains your mind to stay focused on the goals despite distractions and life events that inevitably get in the way. Intentionally state your goals as if you have already achieved them. For example, "I am so happy and grateful now that..." or "I am earning..." or "I am happily married with three kids...." By stating goals in present tense, you are telling the mind a goal is a real object and not just wishful thinking.

   I also suggest posting your goals around your house, on the bathroom mirror, on your office computer, in your journals, and any other place that your eyes may wander throughout the day. This will keep your mind focused on the vision and the goal. Setting clear, measurable goals, stated as facts, feeds the mindset of having intentionality and reaching your goals.

2. **Be Specific:** It is not enough just to jot down a list of goals or intentions. Goals must be in writing and specific. "I want to make six figures" is not specific enough. But "I have earned $100,000 by December 31..." gives the mind clear instructions that this is a real, clear objective you are working toward. If the mind has been given instructions or directedness and has a clear, realistic objective to focus on, it will unconsciously dismiss things that distract you from the objective, and focus on those that move you toward the objective and closer to your well-written, specific intentionality.

3. **Set a Deadline:** Goals stated without a timeline are wishful thinking at best. The mind is an efficient supercomputer that will operate using the programming it came with. It will focus on and execute the prime directive you give it. If you give your mind a specific timeline, it will work efficiently toward the deadline, concentrating all the resources at its disposal to achieve the objective within that timeline. If you miss the deadline, your mind can always be adjusted, but you should never set a goal without intentionality built into the deadline. Set a deadline that challenges you, but is not so difficult to meet that the mind cannot accept it. I would suggest setting a realistic deadline the mind can accept as believable.

4. **Identify Your Plan:** Having a plan to take action will only get you started toward your clear, well-written, specific goals to which you have assigned a challenging, yet realistic deadline. Successful people with highly developed intentionality understand the plan you start with will not be the plan you finish with. Intentionality requires flexibility and adjustments along the way. You must have a plan of action, execute your plan, review and recognize inefficiencies, make changes, and repeat the process over and over until your mind accepts the formula that cracks the code. To guarantee success, it is ultimately your responsibility to adapt and adjust your action plan.

5. **Pay the Price:** It takes sustained effort over a prolonged period to reach your potential and manifest your vision, goals, and dreams. People with well-developed intentionality are hyper-focused on their goals and driven by their dreams and visions. They are relentless in their pursuits and willing to make sacrifices to see their dreams become reality. They borrow from the promise of tomorrow to enroll themselves in today's activities. They align themselves with like-minded individuals who share their passions and willingness to let go of or limit time spent with people who are not going in the same direction. They are willing to pay the price, do the work with enthusiasm, and make the necessary time sacrifices to achieve their dreams and goals.

6. **Say It:** Goals must be reviewed and verbalized daily. I would even suggest going a step further and writing your goals daily before you get out of bed. I know it sounds extreme, but something magical happens when you speak or write goals daily, first thing in the morning. When you wake up, your mind is in alpha state, the state between dreaming and awareness. Alpha state is often referred to as the gateway to the subconscious mind. The vibration or frequency of the mind when in alpha state allows the mind to accept your input without distraction or interruption. When you write or verbalize your goals, you are in creator mode, conditioning your mind to focus on and recognize the positive and the possible. To nurture your intentionality, review, verbalize, and write out your goals daily!

Summary

To achieve your goals, you must first create a vision for your life. The very thought of your vision should inspire you. Your vision should serve as the compass you look to over and over again to evaluate if you are moving toward your vision or away from it.

We often confuse vision with goals. When we fall short of our goals, frustration and disappointment shift our focus away from our vision.

Having a clear, well-defined vision will allow you to continue on course and adjust your goals along the way. Vision is the North Star that guides you. Goals are the benchmarks that need to be accomplished to move to the next level when making your ascent and reaching for your vision.

To stay relevant, we need to realize that vision is more important than goals. When we make the distinction between a vision and goals, we can use short-term and long-term goals as milestones moving in the direction of our ultimate potential.

Action Steps

Write down your vision for your life. Be Specific!

In one year:

_____

_____

In five years:

_____

_____

In ten years:

_____

_____

In twenty years:

_____

_____

Which three things can you do in the next sixty days to help reach your one-year vision?

  1. _____
  2. _____
  3. _____

Which negative beliefs or thoughts not in alignment with your vision are arising and telling you achieving your vision will be difficult or impossible?

  1. _____
  2. _____
  3. _____

Reword those beliefs into positive statements that are in alignment with your vision and support your goals. For example, change, "It requires too much time" to "I know that the investment of a year pursuing this goal will pay dividends for many years to come."

  1. _____
  2. _____
  3. _____

Resources

For additional tools and training, visit TheRelevanceGap.com. To book Scott for an event or consultation, visit ScottScantlin.com. For free tips and motivation, follow him on Twitter and Facebook, and subscribe to his YouTube Channel @ScottScan1.

CHAPTER TWELVE

The Power of Self-Talk

"The brain simply believes what you tell it most. And what you tell it about you, it will create. It has no choice."

— Shad Helmstetter

Jim Kwik, CEO and Founder of Kwik Learning, is a leader in accelerated learning with online students of every age and vocation in more than 150 countries. At the age of five, Jim suffered a head injury that left him struggling in school. He was known as the "boy with the broken brain." For a while, he believed he could never be as good as other kids when it came to learning. Jim was obsessed with superheroes, and when traditional education failed him, Jim's love for comic books kept his dream alive and taught him how to read. Jim vowed one day to find his inner superpower, and he discovered that no matter the circumstances, we can rebuild our brains. His obsession led him to realize his brain was not broken—it just needed a better owner's manual. That journey led Jim to discovering different learning habits, including accelerated learning systems and tactics.

Today, Jim's cutting-edge techniques and impressive mental feats have made him a highly sought-out brain trainer for top entrepreneurs and organizations, with clients around the world, including Zappos, Nike, GE, Fox

Studios, NYU, Harvard, Columbia, Stanford, Singularity, and even companies like SpaceX and Virgin, owned by billionaire geniuses like Richard Branson and Elon Musk.

Jim has become a thought leader in the science of neuroplasticity—the brain's ability to form and reorganize synaptic connections, especially in response to learning or relearning following an injury. Until the latter half of the twentieth century, it was believed the brain developed during a critical period of early childhood and then remained unchanged or static. Research now shows that gray matter can change, synapses can strengthen or weaken over time, and particular brain functions can be transferred to different locations as seen in brain injury cases. Our brain can change the same way we can make programming changes to a computer. As Jim sees it, our brain is like a supercomputer, and our self-talk is the program that runs it.

We are presented the opportunity to change our brains daily through practicing mindfulness, taking captive our thoughts, and becoming aware of our behaviors and emotions. Our negative self-talk originates from the "emotional loops" created during traumatic or stressful experiences. Our very efficient mind ties negative emotions like anger, anxiety, fear, feeling overwhelmed, sadness, or grief to events, and then creates stories around our experiences to protect us from negative emotions. As we encounter similar events, the mind cycles these negative emotions and reinforces thoughts and stories about ourselves to justify the behavior. Over time, these negative thoughts and emotions cycle over and over again, becoming our beliefs about ourselves. In this way, we actually justify our negative self-talk and give ourselves permission to feel good about who we are, and why we do what we do. This process is called activity-dependent plasticity, the biological basis for learning and the formation of new memories.

Our environment also has a significant impact on our self-talk. According to experts, the average toddler hears the word "no" 400 times a day. According to Simon T. Bailey, "By the time a child is 17 years of age, they have heard, 'No,' 150,000 times, and only, 'Yes,' 5,000 times." Bailey says, "The more you continue to hear what you can't do, where you can't go, and who you can't become, there is a neurological path that is created in the brain that causes individuals to shut down."

We are raised in a society where everything is "Stop." Don't do this; don't do that; don't touch that; sit down; that's not yours; give it back; you can't do that! Research now shows we have a mirror neuron—a neuron that fires when we observe the same action performed by others. The story of the five monkeys illustrates this point. The story starts with five monkeys in a cage, with a banana hanging on by a string and a set of stairs leading up to the banana. When one of the monkeys starts up the stairs for the banana, the other monkeys are sprayed with ice-cold water. After a while another monkey makes an attempt, but as soon as his foot touches the ladder, the other monkeys are sprayed again with ice-cold water. It isn't long before the other monkeys physically prevent any monkey from attempting to climb the stairs. At this point, the psychologist performing the experiment shuts off the water because the pattern has been established. One of the original monkeys is also removed and replaced with a new one. As soon as the new monkey goes for the banana, he is violently attacked by the other four. He tries again and is assaulted again. Next, another original is removed and replaced with a newcomer. As soon as the newcomer goes for the banana, he is attacked, and the previous newcomer takes part in the assault with enthusiasm! Likewise, the third, fourth, and fifth monkeys are replaced until there are no more monkeys from the original group. Every time a monkey tries to climb the stairs, he is attacked! After replacing all the original monkeys, none of the newcomers have been sprayed with ice-cold water; nevertheless, no monkey ever again approaches the stairs to try for the banana.

The point of this story is relatively simple. Behavior is learned, and your environment has a significant impact on what you believe you can and cannot do!

You may see this truth about learned behavior at the office, in class, or at the gym. I observe this all the time in my high-intensity interval training (HIIT) training classes. Every morning we go through a warmup; sometimes, the instructor gets distracted or pulled away from leading the group. When this happens, the group looks around at each other and everyone begins to mimic the movements of those closest to them. If left alone for too long, they continue to mimic the moves, even if the steps are incorrect and could possibly cause an injury.

In this same way, we have been conditioned by society to act like others. Along the way, we pick up the beliefs and behaviors of the people closest to us, like our family, friends, neighbors, classmates, coworkers, etc. We are like the five monkeys in the experiment placed into the cage long after the patterning was established. Even though we were never subjected to the ice-cold water, we mirror the behaviors of the others who occupy the same space. In this way, your destiny is tied to the other five monkeys in the cage. If you want the banana, you have to recognize that the banana is not obtainable inside the cage. To get the banana, you have to realize the cage is an illusion. You are living with the outcome of an experiment called social norms. You are caged by a culture that says, "You can't because we can't." This belief is reinforced over time and becomes your belief. Like those who came before us, we assault anyone who violates the norm and justify it so we can feel right about what we believe and who we are.

In the movie *Rise of the Planet of the Apes*, Will Rodman, a scientist at the San Francisco biotech company Gen-Sys, is testing the viral-based drug ALZ-112 on chimpanzees to find a cure for Alzheimer's. ALZ-112 is given to a chimp named Bright Eyes, greatly increasing her intelligence. Bright Eyes gives birth to an infant chimp named Caesar who inherits his mother's intelligence. When Caesar reaches adolescence and sees a dog on a leash like his own, he questions his own identity. Caesar is placed in a primate shelter where he is tormented by the alpha chimp and the chief guard. Caesar learns to unlock his cage, gaining free access to the common area. With the assistance of other apes, he confronts the sanctuary's alpha chimp and claims the alpha position. Caesar eventually escapes the facility, finds canisters of the improved version ALZ-113, and releases the gas, enhancing the other apes' intelligence. When the humans try to get him back into his cage, Caesar speaks for the first time, yelling "No!" The apes release the remaining chimps, flee the facility, and free more apes from the San Francisco Zoo.

This fictional story is an excellent example of the difference between human beings and other primates—awareness! When we become aware of our circumstances, question our identity, and realize we are caged, we want freedom. The difference between other primates and humans is humans can rewire our brains through mindfulness, meditation, and positive self-talk.

When you begin to practice mindfulness, you are taking inventory of your self-talk and beliefs. Beliefs fall into two categories: empowering and disempowering. Empowering beliefs support your dreams, goals, purpose, and aspirations. Disempowering beliefs limit or restrict you from going after your dreams, goals, purpose, or aspirations. Negative self-talk and dis-empowering beliefs start with:

- I can't because....
- I'm too....
- If only I....
- I would but....
- I'm not....
- I don't have....
- My thing is....

Negative self-talk is how we explain away our decision just to be average. These stories are illusions written by our very efficient minds and reinforced by our need for acceptance from others to protect us from the pain we associate with a traumatic experience. In other words, these stories are excuses, lies we tell ourselves and other people so we can justify feeling good about who we are.

I was recently at an event where the trainer had everyone write down on a piece of paper the negative thoughts they were having about how they would not be successful. Then the trainer read the statements, without disclosing who wrote them. They were:

- I'm too short.
- I'm too fat.
- I'm too skinny.
- I'm not tall enough.
- I'm ugly.
- I can't because I have kids.
- I have no free time.
- I'm dumb.
- I can't remember things.
- I'm not a people person.
- I don't think people like me.
- I'm not confident.
- I'm not smart enough.
- I'm afraid to talk to people.
- I'm afraid of rejection.
- I don't want to bother people.

All of these lies are stories our very efficient minds create. They are designed to protect us from something that happened in the early stages of our emotional development called Activity-Dependent Plasticity. These stories are not true; they are an illusion driven by negative emotions and accepted and reinforced by societal norms.

The good news is we can reverse-engineer our experiences and rewrite the stories to convert disempowering beliefs into empowering ones by using Associative-Dependent Plasticity (ADP). ADP is the process of consciously assigning emotions to events, as opposed to activity-dependent plasticity, where emotions are unconsciously assigned. To rewire the mind through ADP, first you need to rewrite your beliefs about negative self-talk. Negative self-talk is like a computer program running in the background directing your behavior as an efficient means of self-preservation. With practice, this process can be done in seconds. As we train the mind by creating new connections and stories about our experiences, our very efficient mind will take over and begin to rewire itself altogether. In this way, our mind becomes our servant, instead of us being a servant to our minds.

Our very efficient minds were designed and conditioned for thousands of years to recognize a threat and keep us safe so we could propagate our species. Like basic programming designed to protect your computer from viruses, your mind believes that the negative self-talk programming it writes about your experiences is keeping you out of danger. Since we no longer face the threat of wild animals, live in caves, or have to hunt and gather food, it is time for us to adapt our minds to today's threats and rewrite our basic programming.

To rewrite our basic programming, we need to develop the practice of mindfulness and awareness of our thoughts, feelings, and emotions. Mindfulness is the practice of taking your thoughts captive and ruling over them. The best way to practice mindfulness is to keep a journal and write down the words and thoughts you are using to express how you feel. Feelings are reactions or beliefs about emotions that have been triggered by an experience. Thoughts are the stories about the emotions we feel or the programming the mind has created to direct our fight-or-flight response.

For example, you start a new business. Making calls to prospective clients is necessary for you to succeed. However, when it comes time to make the calls, you are overwhelmed by fear. You tell yourself, "I can't do this. I'm not a people person. Sales is not for me." At that moment, fear-based emotion takes over and begins to cycle negative self-talk written by the mind based on some experience where you were rejected, felt inadequate, or were made to feel you weren't good enough.

If you run the negative self-talk program, you will fold up and quit. However, if you take it captive, interrupt the basic program, rewrite, and install a new program, you will overcome and be successful.

Emotional Reprogramming/ADP

You can use ADP to interrupt your programming and install a new program. The most effective method for using ADP is meditation. In meditation, we still the mind through breathing exercises. Once we have calmed the mind, we can identify the fear-based emotion associated with the negative self-talk. In this practice, we want to isolate the emotion by separating it from the event.

Fear-based emotions cannot exist within the mind unless they are attached to an event. When you isolate or remove a fear-based emotion from the event that triggered it, it cannot cycle and will dissipate within a minute or two. Once you isolate the emotion, ask your mind to take you back to the emotion's origin. The emotion will stem from a traumatic experience or a stressful situation from the early stages of your emotional development. When you have identified the event, separate the emotion from the event, and allow it to fade away.

Review the stories or negative self-talk about the event, and ask yourself, "Are those stories really true?" As your mind becomes aware that the stories are not true, you will be free to reprogram your mind by rewriting the stories and assigning a new emotion to the event, one that supports the empowering beliefs you have about yourself. Then go back to the current event and assign to it the new emotions and empowering beliefs that support your new state.

Through associative-dependent plasticity, you have rewired your brain. Instead of your mind directing you, you are now directing your mind. Through meditative practice, you have identified the origin of your negative self-talk and changed the source of the event from a threat to a non-threat. Your very efficient mind will no longer run the negative self-talk programming or stories because they are now identified by the mind as untrue. The emotion that has been cycling has been proven false and is no longer available as a valid reference. The negative emotion has been replaced with positive emotion, and the disempowering beliefs with empowering beliefs. From this point forward, your very efficient mind will run the new programming and reinforce the beliefs that support it, over time becoming a part of your subconscious mind. In other words, your new programming will go on auto-pilot, alter your fate, and redirect your destiny.

The Healing Code: Unlock Your Cellular Memory

Another benefit of associative-dependent plasticity is the effect it has on your cellular memory. Alexander Loyd holds doctorates in psychology and naturopathic medicine. His search for a cure for his wife's depression led to the discovery of The Healing Code. In Chapter 2 of his best-selling book *The Healing Code*, he cites a 2004 article, "Medical School Breakthrough," that ran in the *Dallas Morning News* about a research study released by Southwestern University Medical Center. Scientists had discovered that our experiences do not just reside in our brains, but are recorded at the cellular level throughout our bodies, and they believed these cellular memories were the real source of illness and disease.

Loyd states:

Unhealed memories cause stress that holds us back in all areas of life. They deplete our energy, keep us in destructive relationships, and suppress our immune systems. Memory is so much more than we've been traditionally taught. Scientists have proven that our memories are stored, not just in our brains, but throughout our bodies in the form of something we'll call cellular energy. The pain, the trauma, the failure, and the hurt you've experienced can exist in your unconscious mind and memories for years.

On a cellular level, as stated earlier, when our minds identify a threat, the hypothalamus, the part of the brain responsible for our fight-or-flight response, sends a signal throughout the body to shut everything down—nothing in and nothing out. Like a military operation expecting an imminent attack, our very efficient mind is telling our cells to barricade themselves from possible harm by shutting the doors until the threat is gone. The problem with this response is that the cells remain stuck in a fight-or-flight response until the danger is gone.

In other words, negative cellular memories like anger, hate, or resentment cycle throughout our lives, depleting our energy and compromising our immune system, leading to illness and other issues. Fortunately, we now know that by practicing ADP, we can reprogram our epigenetic encoding by replacing negative emotions of fear with positive emotions of love. Exercising ADP releases the cells from the threat and opens them up to receive nutrients and function properly.

All cells need glucose and oxygen for breathing and aerobic respiration. Glucose is a simple sugar made by the body from food; cells use oxygen to break down the glucose to produce the energy for breathing. Carbon dioxide and water are the waste products of respiration that need to be expelled through the lungs. Blood cells are used to transport vital chemicals around the body. When presented with a threat, our epigenetic encoding sends a signal that we need a burst of energy to respond to the situation. We go into a defensive position and lock the cells down. If we never resolve these responses, based on the basic survival programming of our epigenetic encoding, the cells become strongholds that affect every area of our lives.

For example, let's say it is a beautiful day; you are spending time with someone you love and care about deeply. However, during the day, you have a disagreement over something and your feelings get hurt. You mind identifies a potential threat, and your hypothalamus sends a signal throughout your body for your cells to take up a defensive position and that you need a burst of energy to ready yourself for the attack. Your heart races, your palms start to sweat from adrenaline, and you feel like you are going to explode. The mind triggers the emotions from past trauma associated with the thoughts and feelings you are having, and the disagreement turns into a full-blown argument. You are thrown into a fight-or-flight pattern directed by your epigenetic encoding, which is beyond your control. In this way, you go from relationship to relationship, repeating the process until you find someone who either agrees with you or tolerates your programming.

People live their entire lives subjected to a fate beyond their control simply because they cannot control their emotions. Imagine the freedom you would have if you set yourself free from this trap. When you take inventory of your emotions and practice the methods of Associative-Dependent Plasticity, you take control of your emotional state and reprogram your mind with new emotional patterns that support the destiny of your choosing. When you free the mind of negative self-talk and emotions, you are also freeing your cellular memory from the negative memories and emotions stored up throughout your body. When you reprogram your mind to associate positive emotions with a truth that empowers you, cells flow with the energy and vibrancy needed to live the life you've always dreamed about!

Summary

Research now shows our brain can change the same way we can make programming changes to a computer. Our brain is like a supercomputer, and our self-talk is the program that runs it. Our negative self-talk originates from the "emotional loops" created during traumatic or stressful experiences. The good news is we can reverse-engineer our experiences and convert disempowering beliefs into empowering ones. Through the process of Associative-Dependent Plasticity (ADP), we can consciously assign empowering emotions to events that serve us, as opposed to activity-dependent plasticity, where disempowering emotions are unconsciously assigned. Through the practice of Mindfulness Meditation and the Ninety-Second Rule, we can take captive negative self-talk and convert it into positive self-talk that moves us in the direction of our ultimate potential.

Action Steps

Write down three beliefs or thoughts arising in the form of negative self-talk that are not aligned with your vision and goals, and the fear-based emotions associated with them. For example, "I'm not good enough" or "I'm not smart enough" or "I don't want to bother people."

1. _____ Emotion _____

2. _____ Emotion _____

3. _____ Emotion _____

Through the practice of Mindfulness Meditation and the Ninety-Second Rule, identify the root of the "emotional loop" that is driving your behavior; then isolate, release, and reprogram as illustrated in Chapter 7: Emotional Intelligence. Once the root file has been deleted (removed), we can rewrite the experience by attaching an empowering emotion to our experience.

Reword those limiting beliefs into positive self-talk that is in alignment with your vision and supports your goals and the emotions you would like to associate with the story of your experience.

1. _____ Emotion _____

2. _____ Emotion _____

3. _____ Emotion _____

Resources

For additional tools and training, visit TheRelevanceGap.com. To book Scott for an event or consultation, visit ScottScantlin.com. For free tips and motivation, follow him on Twitter and Facebook, and subscribe to his YouTube Channel @ScottScan1.

CHAPTER THIRTEEN

The Path to Your Inherent Ultimate Potential

"Yesterday I was clever, so I wanted to change the world. Today I am wise, so I am changing myself."

— Rumi

When shaping our intentionality, we must take a look at its intrinsic value to set our goals. Life is no longer about survival; we are searching for meaning, for truth. Because survival is all but guaranteed and all our basic needs are meet, existing just to earn a paycheck is no longer enough. If it were, we would quickly lose interest, especially with external motivators losing value.

In 1943, Abraham Maslow introduced the world to his theory of a basic hierarchy of human needs. He published his research in a paper titled, "A Theory of Human Motivation." Known today as "Maslow's Hierarchy of Needs," his theory has influenced how we view human motivation for decades. Often portrayed as a pyramid, Maslow's hierarchy places our most fundamental needs for survival at the bottom and our innate need for self-actualization and expression at the top.

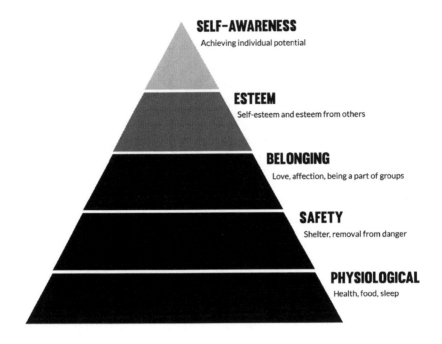

SELF-AWARENESS
Achieving individual potential

ESTEEM
Self-esteem and esteem from others

BELONGING
Love, affection, being a part of groups

SAFETY
Shelter, removal from danger

PHYSIOLOGICAL
Health, food, sleep

Maslow identifies the fundamental four layers (esteem, friendship and love, security, and physical needs) as "deficiency needs" or "d-needs" and the higher level of self-actualization as "being needs" or "b-needs." Deficiency needs drive people to satisfy physiological needs such as hunger, sex, and love; being needs propel people to self-actualization and drive them to fulfill their inherent ultimate potential.

If "deficiency needs" are not met, we experience low-level, fear-based emotions like anxiety and tension. Maslow argues that the basic levels must be met before we can focus on the secondary or higher-level needs of self-actualization and personal expression. Maslow refers to this freedom to express ourselves fully as "meta motivation." When we are not distracted by meeting our basic human needs, we are free to go beyond and reach for our full potential.

Maslow believed a distinction exists between the motivations of those operating below the level of self-actualization and those who are self-actualized and display significant purpose in their work and lives. How many of us have been at the same job for twenty years, are masters at what we do, have our basic needs met, and yet still live without purpose? To compete in the twenty-first century, we must focus on a new set of motivators:

- Who are you?
- Why are you here?
- What are you about?
- What is your purpose?

What if we started with self-awareness and brought the higher-level emotions we want into our daily lives? Instead of living in reaction to low-level emotions like fear, anger, hatred, envy, and anxiety, what if we chose, in advance, high-level emotions like love, peace, joy, competence, acceptance, autonomy, mastery, and purpose that operate in the higher levels of self-actualization? If we change the foundation of our emotional states, we effectively change our daily activities and our overall life experience.

"Aboutness" is an awareness, a state of being. Someone in a state of aboutness knows who they are, where they are going, and why. "Directedness" is seeing yourself as you imagine yourself to be, so much so that your imagined self becomes integrated into every thought and action you take.

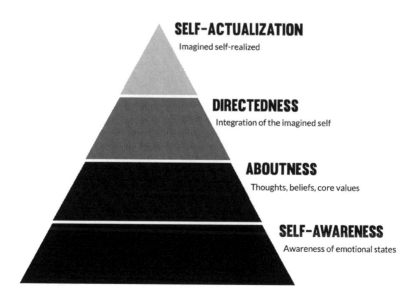

SELF-ACTUALIZATION
Imagined self-realized

DIRECTEDNESS
Integration of the imagined self

ABOUTNESS
Thoughts, beliefs, core values

SELF-AWARENESS
Awareness of emotional states

When setting goals, most of us start by chasing things rather than developing the intentionality that will produce our dream life. We want nice cars, a new house, a loving family, a career we love, financial security, or abundance. The problem with this type of goal setting is we spend most of our time in the present focusing on things we lack, and we quickly lose interest when our goals don't materialize.

I know many successful people who have accomplished everything you could ever imagine, and yet, they are miserable. Why? Though they have acquired everything they have ever wanted, they feel empty. When we chase after things, we assume that money, cars, homes, etc. are going to bring us happiness; however, we quickly realize once we have acquired all of it, that without the emotional states to support our new reality, there is no happiness.

When we push beyond our basic needs into self-actualization, we quickly realize something is missing. More money, more cars, more homes, and new, more prestigious titles are not going to fill the void; we need different motivators. Once a person has successfully navigated the hierarchy of needs, thus satisfying all their basic needs, Maslow suggests they progress to, "A path called growth motivation." This is when being-needs propel a person beyond self-actualization and drive them to fulfill their inherent ultimate potential.

Maslow's hierarchy of needs presents a brilliant picture of the human mind's complexity. The human brain concurrently runs on different levels of motivation. Maslow categorized these needs as relative, general, and primary. Instead of focusing on a specific need at any given time, one need becomes primary as the others remain relative or general. As the primary need is satisfied, a new motivation becomes the dominant need.

Interestingly, this is an excellent illustration of *the relevance gap* that drives us all. Once we have met a need, a gap between where we are and where we could be emerges. Maslow appears to have found the order in which our needs are met, giving us a roadmap for personal development and growth. When we reach one potential, we look to a new possibility, and ultimately, consider our capabilities.

For example, when we start in a new career or embark on a new job, in the beginning, we lack the confidence that comes with experience. However, with proper training and mentorship, we build the confidence necessary to act on our potential. As illustrated in the chart below, every time we act on our potential, we grow in confidence. When we conquer the *gap* we are facing, a new potential emerges. As you reach new levels of potential, you grow in confidence, and your capability expands. Our capacity beyond self-actualization is immeasurable as we press on to new levels and new opportunities.

THE GROWTH GAP

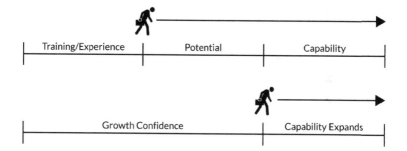

Intrinsic Needs

Above the deficiency needs and the being needs of self-awareness are what I call the intrinsic needs or the "I-needs." When we achieve self-awareness, it can be a little confusing and somewhat uncomfortable. We have been driven and conditioned for years to work at satisfying our deficiency needs when those needs are not fully met, and when we achieve self-awareness, we are left with the thought, *Is this it? Is this really what I want to do?* In other words, do I want to keep spinning the plates that got me here? Obviously, deeper motivators have not been satisfied, and we long for more.

The key to making a successful transition beyond self-actualization to your inherent ultimate potential is to identify your intrinsic motivators and reposition yourself on the path of growth motivation. The first two intrinsic motivators are your *professional awareness* and *personal awareness*.

I once read that successful people always have a personal project. While they are focused and skilled in their profession, they have a side project that brings them great joy. A personal project is, by definition, the essence of intrinsic motivation. There is no external reward; it is something you do just for the joy of doing it. It is something you have longed for all of your life, and you perform the tasks associated with your personal project with pure joy. You can work on it for hours and lose track of time. It is essential when you reach self-actualization to transition into your personal project. When you have a personal project, it gives you the freedom to appreciate who you are as a professional.

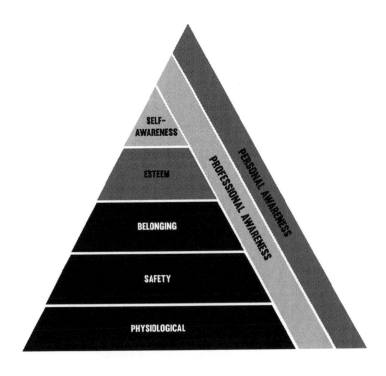

Eventually, your personal project will fuel your identity and spill over into your professional life. When this happens, you will move to the next level on your growth path and develop your capacity for empathy. Because you have experienced all the emotions associated with every level of growth, you have an understanding and an awareness of, and you are sensitive to, all the various experiences related to your path. Because you have experienced all the feelings, thoughts, and emotions, you have developed emotional intelligence and can objectively help others overcome their limiting beliefs and emotions. In other words, you will stand in the gap and assist others in making the ascent as you did.

As you begin to identify potential all around you, and help others to make each transition from deficiency needs to self-actualization and beyond, you will be admired for your aboutness and directedness and how they have brought you to personhood—becoming someone admired by all, whom we all aspire to be.

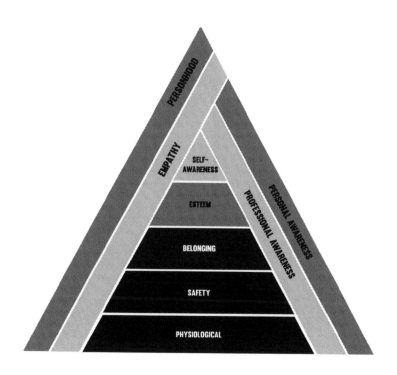

Helping others succeed and find their purpose is our inherent ultimate potential. At this stage of development, you have reached personhood. You are a role model, an example of what's possible, and you have significant influence over others. It is your obligation and duty to give what you have received, freely, and you do so gladly. With all of your basic needs met, you can see clearly, and your priorities shift away from serving self to serving others.

With an intentionality mindset, we are always aware of *the relevance gap*, the gap between where we are and where we could be. Each level of the hierarchy of needs presents a new challenge of growth and possibility. We are either expanding or contracting; there is no room for complacency with intentionality.

Summary

Maslow argues that our basic needs (deficiency needs) must be met before we can focus on the secondary or higher-level needs of self-actualization and personal expression. When we are not distracted by meeting our basic human needs, we are free to go beyond and reach for our ultimate potential. However, when we push beyond our basic needs into self-actualization, we quickly realize something is missing. Interestingly, this is an excellent illustration of the relevance gap that drives us all. Once we have met a need, a gap between where we are and where we could be emerges. To stay relevant and compete, we must never lose sight of the gap. When we reach one potential, we look to a new possibility, and ultimately, consider our capabilities.

Action Steps

Make a list of three things you can do this year that will move you up the scale to your next level of potential. Then rank the list—number one being the scariest, number three being the least scary. Then start with the least scary. Once you knock that one down, your confidence will grow and you can go after the second one. Once you knock that one down, your confidence will become even stronger and you can go after the scariest of the three.

1. _____
2. _____
3. _____

Resources

For additional tools and training, visit TheRelevanceGap.com. To book Scott for an event or consultation, visit ScottScantlin.com. For free tips and motivation, follow him on Twitter and Facebook, and subscribe to his YouTube Channel @ScottScan1.

CHAPTER FOURTEEN

Changing Our Preference and Patterns

"The world as we have created it is a process of our thinking. It cannot be changed without changing our thinking."

— Albert Einstein

In business, sports, or any field where you strive to succeed, there is a promise you will receive if you commit to working hard and putting in the hours. This intrinsic motivation drives you to take risks, get out of your comfort zone, and do things you otherwise would not do if there were not a promise—a deep need to see it through, and an opportunity to obtain your prize. This promise may be the fulfillment of a lifelong dream, an education or degree, residual income, time freedom, or the ability to live life on your own terms. Whatever the promise you so greatly desire to achieve, when there is a promise, you develop a "whatever it takes" mindset; then you are willing to make the necessary sacrifices to see it through and obtain your just reward.

When there is a promise, you operate entirely on faith, believing that all your hard work and sacrifice will pay off. You have been bitten by the bug, you have drank the Kool-Aid, and you are prepared to do whatever it takes to accomplish your end goal. Although there are external rewards, you are operating entirely on intrinsic motivation. You may not be making much progress, but the overwhelming emotions of significance and accomplishment are so intoxicating that they create tunnel vision, and you will do anything to feel that emotion over and over again.

Your Preferences

The challenge you face is that you have to overcome your preferences to achieve and reach your promise. Here is where most people bail; they are unwilling to break away from their preferences. For example, in business, you will be required to do and master:

- Prospecting
- Making calls
- Hosting meetings
- Following up
- Asking for the sale
- Facing rejection

Despite all of your best efforts, you may find it difficult to do these things. When you are in a fear-based state, you will default to the emotions of past experiences, which are designed to protect you from feelings associated with failure and rejection. These fear-based emotions stand between you and your promise. Just because you have a promise doesn't mean you have the right mindset or intentionality to obtain success. Intentionality takes time to develop, and your promise will require that you change your thoughts, opinions, and beliefs if you want to change your lifestyle.

The Pattern

Your preferences are the day-to-day habits or patterns you have developed, adopted, or inherently received from the generations that came before you. These patterns wield some kind of invisible force over you, causing you to withdraw from the activity or pursuit of your promise. It shows up in your:

- Self-talk
- Justifications for your actions
- Excuses

This invisible prison is the reason most people never succeed. Their preprogrammed epigenetics and imprints from their environment are directing their fight-or-flight responses and reinforcing old patterns that stand in the way of success. This is why we see people at conferences year after year buying the programs, reading the books, and getting the training but never having a breakthrough. We essentially become personal development junkies because we are chasing a feeling, but without real transformation, you will never reach your desired outcome. If you want the promise, you have to replace old patterns with new ones—patterns to achieve your desired outcome or intentionality.

Fortunately, new patterns are all around you. Your first step is to acknowledge that success is not subject to your preferences. There are patterns that work and patterns that don't work. Once you have accepted this fact, you can model successful people and adopt their patterns to achieve your desired outcome.

The Law of Disappointment

Our faith usually grows when it is tested by disappointments. We spend all of our time trying to figure out how we think things should be done based on our own expectations or preferences. When our expectations do not match up with our preferences, we face discouragement and want to give up. That is when we need to realize the opportunity for breakthrough and growth is before us. Based on how we respond to discouragement, we will either strengthen or weaken our faith.

At the point of discouragement is an underlying program directing your fight-or-flight response. Your mind does not have a reference for overcoming the emotion you are experiencing, so it is running a program based on past experiences designed to protect you. It doesn't matter how many books you read, seminars you attend, or training sessions you go to, this program is going to run, and it is going to override everything you know unless you reprogram your emotional response and the story it is attached to.

Exercising the Ninety-Second Rule

If you want to experience radical transformation, you need to exercise the Ninety-Second Rule: *An emotion, good or bad, cannot exist if it is not attached to a story*. For example, discouragement is a fear-based emotion attached to past experience; it is designed to protect you from feelings associated with discouragement like self-pity, depression, or loss. Through the practice of Mindfulness Meditation, you can isolate the feeling of discouragement and revisit the story of when you first experienced the disappointment that is driving your behavior.

During meditation, you can exercise the Ninety-Second Rule by separating the emotion from the story. By isolating the emotion, it cannot exist and will dissolve in less than ninety seconds.

When I say dissolve, I mean it literally. Emotions are made up of chemicals that activate when the fight-or-flight response is triggered. When you separate the emotion from the story, the chemicals that make up the feeling of discouragement literally dissolve out of your bloodstream and are no longer available to trigger your mind's response to your present experience. You will need to run this pattern over and over again, each and every time you want to quit or give up. You will be pleased to find that only a handful of past experiences stand in your way. Once these roadblocks are removed, you will experience a lasting transformation that will serve you for years to come.

Yes, in the eyes of God we are all equal, but we are not all alike in the cards we have been dealt. While some find life effortless and succeed quickly, most of us need to address our epigenetics and imprintations and do the emotional work if we are going to experience true transformation and live the lives we dream of.

The first step of growth is overcoming disappointments and expectations. If you resist the urge to control the outcome with your existing preferences, identify fear-based emotions that are holding you back, and replace them with new patterns and emotions that free you from your invisible prison, your business will flourish.

Summary

The promise of our potential drives us to take risks, get out of our comfort zone, and do things we otherwise would not do had the promise not been there. When we consider the benefits of reaching our potential, we develop a "whatever it takes" mindset and we are willing to do what is necessary to see it through. The challenge we face is that we have to overcome our preferences to achieve and reach our promise. Just because we have promise doesn't mean we have the right mindset to achieve it. If we want to stay relevant, we have to replace old patterns with new ones—patterns that will move us toward our desired outcome or ultimate potential.

Action Steps

Make a list of expectations or preferences that may be holding you back from your potential. For example, "I hate technology" or "If I have to talk to people, I can't do it" or "I don't use social media."

1. _____

2. _____

3. _____

Use the practice of Mindfulness Meditation and the Ninety-Second Rule to isolate, release, and program new, empowering emotions and preferences that will move you toward your ultimate potential. Make a list of your new empowering preferences and review them daily.

1. _____

2. _____

3. _____

Resources

For additional tools and training, visit TheRelevanceGap.com. To book Scott for an event or consultation, visit ScottScantlin.com. For free tips and motivation, follow him on Twitter and Facebook, and subscribe to his YouTube Channel @ScottScan1.

CHAPTER FIFTEEN

Winning the Race for Relevance

"When writing the story of your life, don't let anyone else hold the pen."

– Harley Davidson

We have all heard that doing the same thing repeatedly and expecting a different result is the definition of insanity. Today, *doing the same things repeatedly and expecting things to stay the same is what's crazy!* To win the race for relevance in your business or career, you must acknowledge that change is not going to slow down. Things are not going to go back to the way they always were. Wishing things would go back to how they used to be is dangerous. You can no longer afford to neglect the change.

To move forward in the race for relevance, you must embrace your limitations. Your potential is hidden in your limitations—that's where the growth is! If you are struggling with technology, mobile devices, apps, or social media platforms like YouTube, Facebook, Instagram, or Twitter, online courses are readily available and much more affordable than going back to college. For a few hundred bucks, or a *free* YouTube tutorial, you can master those tools in the evening or over the weekend.

To win the race for relevance, you must adopt the right mindset and develop your intentionality. If you struggle with negative self-talk or limiting core values, or have you lost sight of your potential, then use the tools and the training you have learned in this book to shift your thinking and reprogram your mind to move you toward your ultimate potential.

Through the practice of Mindfulness Meditation and the Ninety-Second Rule, you will develop the skills necessary to consciously shift your experience and rewrite your story with empowering emotions that will move you toward the outcomes you desire. In time, these principles and habits will become second nature and propel you toward radical transformational change.

To stay relevant, you need to create a vision for your life that lines up with your personal values and will lift up the world around you. Harley Davidson once wrote, "When writing the story of your life, don't let anyone else hold the pen." Decide what you want to do and go after it because years will go by and you will look back and ask yourself what you actually did. I can't imagine anything worse than looking back and knowing that I didn't go for it because I was afraid of what other people would think.

Most people are afraid to try again. They think about what happens if it doesn't work. If they fail again, what will people think? Steve Jobs said in a commencement speech to the graduating class at Stanford University, "Don't be trapped by dogma, which is living with the results of other people's thinking. Don't let the noise of others' opinions drown out your own inner voice." If your vision is big enough, if you have created a clear picture of who you are and what you are about, then it doesn't matter what other people think. Your vision is everything. It's your North Star, your guiding light.

A FINAL NOTE

Do More Than Read This Book

Now that you have finished *The Relevance Gap*, what actions are you going to take? What goals are you going to set? What vision are you going to create? What changes are you going to make?

I challenge you to review the summaries and action steps at the end of each chapter and take action! Knowledge is not power; *applied* knowledge is power. You can read all the books in this world, but if you don't apply the techniques and skills described in those books, you will never achieve your inherent ultimate potential.

On the ten lines below, list ten actions you will commit to taking within the next ninety days, in response to reading this book.

1. _____
2. _____
3. _____
4. _____
5. _____
6. _____
7. _____
8. _____
9. _____
10. _____

If you apply the steps and principles that are laid out in this book you will rediscover your potential and bridge the *gap* from where you are to where you could be. You will overcome that feeling of falling behind and find a sense of certainty and confidence that you matter, you belong, and you can make a difference. Then you will be on your way to becoming the best version of yourself you were destined to be.

Now that you have read my book, I encourage you to hit me up on your favorite social media platform with a message followed by #TheRelevance-Gap, and I will know that you have read my book. On Twitter, Facebook, YouTube, or LinkedIn, I am @ScottScantlin (or just search for "Scott Scant-lin"). Tell me what you liked about my book and what I could have done better so I can improve it for the next printing. More importantly, tell me about you, your challenges, your obstacles and adversities so I can help you.

In fact, I would like to offer you a complimentary, no-obligation thir-ty-minute consultation by phone, web-meeting (Zoom, Skype, GoToMeet-ing, StartMeeting), or in person (if geography allows) to see how I can help and assist you. To book your thirty-minute, no-obligation consultation, visit ScottScantlin.com.

I wish you good luck! I wish you prosperity! I wish you all the success in the world....

Your friend,

L. Scott Scantlin

RESOURCES

TheRelevanceGap.com

Please visit this website for additional tools and training illustrated in *The Relevance Gap*.

ScottScantlin.com

Please visit this site to book Scott for an event or to schedule a consultation. Whether delivering a keynote to your organization, using our training materials, speaking at your church or school, or delivering a virtual seminar to your people, Scott would love the privilege to coach and serve you.

For Free Tips And Motivation, Follow Scott!

Twitter @ScottScantlin
Facebook: /ScottScan1
YouTube: /ScottScan1

ABOUT THE AUTHOR

Scott Scantlin is a professional speaker, author, consultant, sales trainer, and business coach with two decades of experience in direct sales and leadership. He successfully built a nationwide team of over 6,000 independent associates across North America and Canada. He has served in high level leadership roles and specializes in working with companies, entrepreneurs, and direct sellers both individually and corporately to identify hidden potential and reach for their very best. A lifelong student of personal development, Scott wrote The Relevance Gap to help those struggling to transition during a time of extreme change. He currently resides in Kansas City, Missouri, with his wife Kimberly, and their two dogs, Junie and Bell.

An active philanthropist, Scott will donate a portion of the proceeds from this book to The Global Orphan Project.

To meet him, go to ScottScantlin.com.

Made in the USA
Lexington, KY
26 November 2019

57701750R00096